Centre for Reformation and Renaissance Studies

University of Toronto

Translation Series   4

Nicholas of Cusa

The Layman
on Wisdom and the Mind

Translated, with an Introduction and Notes, by

M. L. Führer

Dovehouse Editions Canada

1989

Canadian Cataloguing in Publication Data

Nicholas, of Cusa, Cardinal, 1401–1464
    The layman on wisdom and the mind

(Renaissance and Reformation texts in translation;   4)
Translation of: Idiota de sapientia et de mente.
Includes bibliographical references.

ISBN 0–919473–56–3

1. Intellect—Early works to 1800. 2. Cognition—Early works
to 1800. 3. Knowledge, Theory of—Early works to 1800.
I. Führer, M. L. (Markus Lorenz). II. Title. III. Series.

B765.N53I4413   1989   128'.2   C88–090431–3

For information on distribution or for placing orders write to:
    Dovehouse Editions Inc.
    32 Glen Avenue
    Ottawa, Canada
    K1S 2Z7

For further information about the series write to:
    The Editors, Renaissance and Reformation texts in translation
    Centre for Reformation and Renaissance Studies
    Victoria University in the University of Toronto
    Toronto, Canada, M5S 1K7

Typeset by the HUMANITIES PUBLICATION CENTRE, University of Toronto.

Printed in Canada by Imprimerie Gagné Ltée.

Contents

"They claim, however, that I am altogether illiterate, that I am a plain uneducated fellow." —Petrarch

Preface

The translation of Nicholas of Cusa's *Idiota de sapientia et de mente* is based upon Ludwig Baur's critical edition that appears as volume five of the Heidelberg Academy edition of Cusanus' *Opera omnia*. It was printed in Leipzig in 1937 by Felix Meiner Verlag. The work also appears in a number of early printed editions, including the Paris edition of 1514, the Basel edition of 1563, and the Strasbourg edition of 1488. The work survives in twenty-six manuscripts. Dr. Baur lists and discusses all of them in the introduction to his edition of the *Idiota*. It is important to notice that one of these manuscripts is extant in Cusanus' own library that is housed in the Cusanus Hospital in Bernkastl, Germany. This work, codex cusanus 218, along with four other manuscripts (codices norimbergensis V–72, oenipontanus 444, wratislaviensis IQ 97, and islebensis 960) form the principal basis for Baur's edition.

There are only a few places in the translation where I take exception with the critical edition in favour of alternate readings. These deviations from the critical text are marked by a note indicating the alternate reading. In preparing this translation, I have followed the following eight principles. First, I use a single word wherever possible to express a Latin term. Second, the Latin text is never paraphrased but always presented as literally as possible without sacrificing the sense of the English translation. Third, all ambiguous expressions are noted and possible renderings suggested. Fourth, all special renderings, particularly of technical terms, are noted. Fifth, the reader is referred to Cusanus' possible sources wherever such a reference is needed to grasp the intention of the text. Sixth, the original Latin is always cited for peculiar renderings. Seventh, alternate readings from the critical text are always noted. Eighth, obscure references or allusions that may require special information not presumed in a modern reader are always explained.

I wish to thank my college for providing me with a leave of absence in order to prepare this translation. And I particularly wish to express my gratitude to Professor F. Edward Cranz of Connecticut College for giving so graciously of his time and skills in reading through my translation and making suggestions. Any defects in the final rendering must be understood by the reader to be due to the weakness of my own intellect and not to the eminent advice of my learned mentor and friend. Lastly, I wish to thank my students at Augsburg College who used handouts of the drafts of this work for their comments and suggestions that have hopefully made this rendition more readable to all students in their quest for understanding Nicholas of Cusa.

Introduction

Nicholas of Cusa was born in 1401 at Kues, in Germany. His family name was Krebs but he has come to be known as Nicholas of Cusa or simply Cusanus, after the Latinized form of Kues. Concerning his early life little is known. In 1416, however, he matriculated at Heidelberg University and studied for one year. He then attended the University of Padua where he studied Canon Law, receiving the degree of doctor in 1423. Upon returning to Germany, he went to the University of Cologne in order to continue his studies in theology. Later he became secretary to Ulrich von Manderscheid, whom he represented in a legal matter at the Council of Basel. In 1435 he was offered an academic appointment at the University of Louvain but he declined it. Instead, he pursued a career as an ecclesiastic. In 1448 he was made a cardinal of the Church, his titular parish being S. Pietro in Vincoli. Pope Nicholas V appointed Cusanus Bishop of Brixen in Tyrol in 1450. This appointment led him into a bitter struggle, lasting nearly up to his death, with Duke Sigismund of Austria over problems of church reform. Between the years 1451 and 1452 Cusanus acted as papal nuncio to Germany. Later he became the Pope's vicar general in Rome. He died at Todi in 1464 while carrying out his papal duties. His body was buried in his titular church in Rome, but his heart was removed and taken to Kues.

Cusanus' writings reveal a man who, although engaged in political affairs, was deeply philosophical. As many other figures of the Renaissance, he was learned in a wide range of studies, including philosophy, law, medicine, theology, mathematics, and mechanics. In writing about these subjects, he develops methods of thought and styles of composition that are different from those of many of his contemporary scholastics. He often uses the dialogue form, introduces mathematical analogies, and proceeds directly to his topic without the usual dialectical structure of the traditional medieval *quaestio*. It would be an error, however, to assume that Cusanus' thought is totally modern. For he is in many respects the heir to a medieval tradition in German thought that can be traced back to St. Albert the Great through such figures as Ulrich of Strasbourg, Dietrich of Freiberg, Berthold of Mosburg,

Meister Eckhart, and Heinrich Suso. These thinkers developed a theology that was profoundly mystical and Cusanus' writings manifest their influence.

The mystical dimension in Cusanus' writings is revealed in the work that he entitled the *Idiota* and which we render into English as *The Layman*. In fact, the term *idiota* presents the translator with his first problem. For it does not strictly mean a layman; it seems to require some kind of modifier such as "simple layman" or "uneducated layman." Indeed, it is difficult to decide which adjective is appropriate because the term is unique in meaning. Consequently, it is almost beyond the compass of an English equivalent. The term in Latin is a transliteration of the Greek word *Idiotes*, which means a private man, a free man, or a man lacking an education. In Latin the term came to refer to anyone possessing no science or discipline, as well as to a simple man. During the Middle Ages, however, especially with the rise of monasticism, the term took on a spiritual meaning. This new meaning seems to have been motivated by passages in Scripture. The key passage is found in the *Acts of the Apostles* (IV, 13): "Now seeing the boldness of Peter and John, and finding that they were uneducated and ordinary men (*sine litteris et idiotae*), they began to marvel, and to recognize them as having been with Jesus." Jean Leclercq, in his study of medieval monasticism, *L'Amour des lettres et le désir de Dieu*,[1] points out that monastic culture tended to construe this kind of passage in terms of spiritual humility, as opposed to intellectual pride. The monk as *idiota* perceived himself as applying his mind to a single purpose and eschewed the multiplication of questions that dominated the minds of the learned. He saw himself as pursuing a kind of holy integrity that vain knowledge could destroy by instigating the vice of pride in the intellect. Only if the mind was simple and unified could it be prepared to contemplate its Creator, who is likewise simple and one. The *idiota* therefore came to adopt what might be called a "spiritual boldness," which the passage cited from Scripture seemed to indicate as being the result of "having been with Jesus."

Ought we then to translate *idiota* as "layman," when the first type of *idiota* seems to have been the medieval monastic? By the fifteenth century, however, the monastic was no longer the sole exemplar of holy simplicity. A new movement, a movement of lay piety called the *devotio moderna*, had come into existence. Not unlike its monastic antecedent, it too detested the endless controversies of the schoolmen and feared the inflation of the pride of excessive learning. It must be pointed out, however, that the *idiota* of the *devotio moderna* was not understood as being confined exclusively to the laity. The monastic ideal was extended into lay culture, but not at the expense of monastic culture. The protagonist of Cusanus' dialogue is clearly a layman. In fact he is a woodcarver. He seems to represent the ideal of the *devotio moderna* insofar as he confounds the foolishness and pride of the orator and instructs the philosopher in the doctrine of the divinity of the mind.

While it is true that Cusanus' *idiota* is a simple layman, the adjective "simple" should be understood in its medieval spiritual sense. It is also true that this layman is uneducated, in the sense that he is not a product of the schools of rhetoric or philosophy. But he is wise and he knows the ways of the mind to a degree that amazes both the philosopher and the orator. He possesses the kind of spiritual boldness mentioned earlier. So we shall refer to him and to Cusanus' dialogue as simply "the layman" and ask the reader to bear in mind the history and meaning of the term *idiota*.

Cusanus composed *The Layman* in 1450. The manuscript tradition usually describes four books or divisions of the work: two books on wisdom, one book on the mind, and a final book on experiments with weights. There is a particular unity that marks the first three books of the dialogue. This unity could perhaps best be described as Augustinian because it was St. Augustine who declared that he wanted to know only two things—God and the soul. The first two books of the dialogue deal with wisdom. The classical definition of wisdom, found in Cicero and repeated in St. Augustine, is that wisdom is the "knowledge of things human and divine." Perhaps it is from this definition that St. Augustine determines the two objects of his intellectual desire, God and the soul. It is apparent in Cusanus' dialogue that wisdom is understood in a Christian sense. It is identified with the Holy Trinity and in particular with the Second Person of the Trinity. Christ is that Wisdom through which the mind comes to know God.

The object of the first two books of the dialogue concerns the contemplation of God. The layman instructs an orator in the traditional threefold path of mysticism: purgation, illumination, and perfect contemplation. The purgative element is handled early in the first book. The layman confronts the eloquent orator with the spiritual boldness of the monastic *idiota*. He instructs him in humility and warns him about the dangers of intellectual pride. Then he quickly turns to the theme of illumination, revealing to the orator the paradox of wisdom: quoting from the *Book of Proverbs* he declares that "Wisdom cries out in the streets." This, he tells the orator, means that wisdom is accessible to all men who will but look to see it. Yet the *Book of Ecclesiasticus* reveals that Wisdom "dwells in the highest." This passage is interpreted to mean that there is a hiddenness about God that man in his finitude cannot conceive. Here we find Cusanus repeating a theme from an earlier work, *On Learned Ignorance*. Man is called to know God, but it is a "hidden God" that he is called to know. In order to know such a God, man must first purge himself of the attitude of false learning, which is the belief that by finite modes he can comprehend a hidden deity that is infinite. He must realize his ignorance before he can grasp that the only knowledge he can have of God is negative.

The development of learned ignorance in the human soul is presented by Cusanus in *On Learned Ignorance* as an act of intellectual purgation. He clarifies and expands this doctrine in *The Layman* by suggesting the traditional distinction between God understood as *deus* and as *deitas*. According to this distinction, which Cusanus might have found in Meister Eckhart, the God that cries out in the streets as wisdom is *deus*, the God who reveals Himself. But the God that He reveals is the *deitas*, the deity Himself, the hidden Godhead. The paradox is that the Godhead is revealed as being hidden. Cusanus' use of the *deus-deitas* distinction is important for two reasons. First, it clarifies the fact that Cusanus is thinking within the medieval mode of *fides quaerens intellectum*, faith seeking understanding. He is not trying to establish any system of proofs for the existence of God or the divine attributes, as one critic incorrectly maintains.[2] He is operating within the context of faith and is seeking to understand what he finds revealed there. Second, the revelation of wisdom crying out in the streets is a beautiful reaffirmation of the old medieval image of the book of nature complementing the book of Sacred Scripture. Here Cusanus is following St. Augustine's *De doctrina christiana*, which teaches that things in the mundane order are taken as signs for things in the divine order. Nature is a book wherein the soul can read about God. Because of man's fallen nature, however, he cannot read this book without special help from God. At this point Cusanus affirms the traditional doctrine of mystical illumination. The appearance in his text of the term "field of virtues" refers to the virtues that are infused into the soul at the end of the purgative phase of the mystical way. This infusion is the work of the *deus* who reveals himself in the streets. He is the wisdom who leads the soul from the perception of the external world, by means of its faculty of discretion, to the realization of the absolute unity of the

Godhead, by means of the intellect.

The second book of the dialogue on wisdom is an extensive treatment of the hiddenness of God. Following Meister Eckhart, Cusanus explains the relationship between God and the intellect, or mind. He then proceeds to show that the Second Person of the Trinity, who is Wisdom, must be understood as equivalent to mind. This divine mind expresses itself, as all minds do, in words. For the Second Person of the Trinity, the expression of the divine mind, is the Word, the divine *logos* that contains the forms of all things.

At this point in the dialogue Cusanus introduces another theme from *On Learned Ignorance*, which he calls the "coincidence of opposites." This doctrine constitutes Cusanus' version of the third phase in the mystical way. The soul contemplates the mystery of the Godhead as the coincidence of two opposite concepts that the mind constructs to define it. Cusanus maintains that it is appropriate to understand the Godhead as that which cannot be greater than it is. At the same time, it cannot be understood as being less than it is. Therefore, the Absolute, the Godhead, is both the maximum and the minimum.

The first two books of *The Layman* deal with the mystical approach to God; the third book is concerned with the soul as mind. It presents an orderly analysis of mind in which the influence of St. Augustine's *De quantitate animae* is present in many of the questions that Cusanus raises. The book proceeds from a definition of the mind as a function of the soul through an analysis of God as mind and man as the image of God to a discussion of the immortality of the mind. Having established a Neoplatonic distinction between mind and soul in which the mind is a divine-like transcendent dimension of the soul, not dependent upon the body for its existence, Cusanus develops an extensive analysis of the relation of the human mind as the image of God to God and creation. Just as God creates the world through the divine mind, man recreates it through the assimilative power of his finite mind. Here Cusanus is repeating the Neoplatonic theme of the procession of creatures from the mind of God and their return to God through man's act of mental assimilation.

Cusanus introduces a new interpretation of the traditional doctrine of the mind as the image of God when he insists that this image is active. It is not a passive mirror-like reflection of creation and hence of the Creator; it is active in its own right. It is perhaps here that Cusanus' dialogue had its greatest influence upon the Renaissance. For the theme of the mind as a kind of miniature divinity in which ideas can be assimilated as well as imposed is one found in writers such as Pico della Mirandola, Marsilio Ficino, Leonardo da Vinci, and Giordano Bruno.

Throughout the entire discussion of the mind we can observe Cusanus struggling with the teachings of Meister Eckhart concerning the divinity of the human mind. The issue becomes critical in chapter twelve where Cusanus rejects the Averroistic thesis of the unity of the intellect. While he agrees with Eckhart that the creative ability of the mind makes man the image of God, indeed the highest image in creation, Cusanus stops short of identifying God and the human mind as having parity in the order of being. Throughout the remainder of the dialogue Cusanus insists that the divine aspect of the human mind is found in the order of the soul's perfection, which is the last phase of the mystical way. Man can come to *reflect* God more and more as he is illuminated by the divine exemplars, and this reflection is active and not passive. But the mind cannot ever become God. In the state of contemplative perfection, however, there will be no way of distinguishing the divine from the perfected human mind in terms of content, because the human mind will have the same ideas as the divine mind.

F. P. Pickering has shown in his article, "Notes on Late Medieval German Tales in Praise of *Docta Ignorantia*," that works such as Cusanus' dialogue constitute a genre of literature popular in Germany at the close of the Middle Ages. "This type of tale," he argues, "must be familiar to anyone acquainted with the popular mystic literature of the later Middle Ages in Germany. But it is naturally to be found in other contexts: it may well be an evergreen theme in religious writings that a simple layman may, in respect of true piety, excel one in holy orders."[3] It is of course true that Cusanus' layman is not merely pious, nor does he confront anyone in holy orders. But Pickering identifies the genre correctly when he determines that it belongs to the mystic tradition. Cusanus' innovation is his addition of the order of knowledge to piety. In many respects, Cusanus' *The Layman* seems to be an amalgamation of the genre Pickering describes and themes from Petrarch's *De sui ipsius et multorum ignorantia*. Interestingly enough, a later work, entitled *De vera sapientia*, was attributed to Petrarch, but seems to be modelled on Cusanus' dialogue. Cusanus also seems to have been influenced by some of the writings of Ramon Lull. Lull not only developed a refined type of the layman, but dealt with the mind in a number of ways that must have influenced Cusanus. His emphasis on the analogies of mind and number appear many times in Cusanus' dialogue.

While Cusanus' work has definite precedents, it also has a progeny. Leonardo da Vinci, for example, paraphrases in his *Il codice Atlantico* the opening words of Cusanus' dialogue in order to establish the primacy of experience. Carolus Bovillus, the sixteenth-century French theologian, responds directly in his *De sapiente* to Cusanus' analysis of wisdom and the mind. The use that both of these thinkers made of *The Layman* reveals that Cusanus' dialogue is not totally a Renaissance document. Da Vinci identifies experience with wisdom; his concern is with the empirical and the mathematical. The mystical strain in Cusanus is lost on him. Bovillus, perhaps the true heir to Cusanus' mysticism, rejects Cusanus' distinction between wisdom and knowledge. He accepts the common Renaissance premise that wisdom is the product of knowledge. According to Cusanus' more medieval view, wisdom is acquired by grace and imposed on experience, enlightening thereby the Book of Nature. Cusanus' position, therefore, is not one that is typical of the Renaissance. He is not interested in the empirical method nor in experience for its own sake. His thinking moves away from the world to the contemplation of the divine mind and the immortality of the human mind in its vision of God. Yet his methodology and style of writing, which has already been described as being neither scholastic nor typically medieval, deeply influenced many Renaissance thinkers. *The Layman*, therefore, is a book that is very much a product of the transitional character of fifteenth-century thought in Germany: it looks back to the Middle Ages for its doctrine and forward to the Renaissance for its method of analysis.

BOOK I

The Layman on Wisdom

A certain poor Layman met a very rich Orator in the Roman forum. Smiling pleasantly, he addressed him as follows:

LAYMAN: I am astonished at your pride. Wearied by the constant reading of countless books, you are not led to humility.[1] No doubt this is because the knowledge of this world, in which you believe that you excel all others, is foolishness with God and puffs men up.[2] True knowledge, however, humbles them. I wish that you would apply yourself to this kind of knowledge because it is the treasury of gladness.[3]

ORATOR: What presumption is this, that you, a poor and completely ignorant layman, should despise the study of letters,[4] without which no one makes progress?[5]

LAYMAN: Great orator, it is not presumption but love that forbids me to remain silent. For I see that you are dedicated to the search for wisdom, but with much useless labour. If I am able to recall you from this, in such a way that you too could consider it an error, I believe that you would rejoice at your escape from a common trap.[6] The opinion of authority has distracted you. As a result you are like a horse, free by nature, but bound fast with a halter to a manger where it eats only what is given to it. Your intellect, fettered to the authority of writers, is fed strange and unnatural foods.[7]

ORATOR: Where is the food of wisdom, if not in the books of wise men?

LAYMAN: I do not say that it is not there, but that it is not there naturally. Those men who first applied themselves to writing about wisdom did not receive an increase of wisdom from the food of books that did not yet exist. They attained perfect manhood by natural nourishment.[8] And they by far exceed others who think that they have advanced by books.

ORATOR: Some things can be known without the study of letters, but not difficult and great things because the sciences have increased through additions.[9]

LAYMAN: That is what I said; you are led by authority and are deceived. Someone has written the opinion that you believe. But I tell you that wisdom cries out in the streets, and her cry is that she dwells in the highest.[10]

ORATOR: From what I hear, although you are a layman, you think that you are wise.

LAYMAN: The difference between us is maybe that you think that you are knowledgeable even though you are not. Hence you are proud. I know for a fact that I am a layman. In this I am humbled. Perhaps I am more learned for that reason.

ORATOR: Being a layman, how are you able to come to the knowledge of your ignorance?[11]

LAYMAN: Not from your books, but from God's.[12]

ORATOR: What books are those?

LAYMAN: The ones that He has written with His own finger.[13]

ORATOR: Where are they found?

LAYMAN: Everywhere.

ORATOR: Even in this forum?

LAYMAN: Yes indeed. I have already said that wisdom cries out in the streets.

ORATOR: I wish to hear how.

LAYMAN: If I saw that your desire is not due to mere curiosity, I would reveal great things to you.

ORATOR: Can you do this briefly in order that I may get a taste of what you mean?

LAYMAN: Yes, I can.

ORATOR: Then let us go into this barber's shop where we may sit and you can speak more quietly.

This suggestion pleased the Layman, and, upon entering the place, they turned to face the forum. The Layman began the discourse as follows:

LAYMAN: I shall attempt to demonstrate to you what I told you, namely that wisdom cries out in the streets, and her cry is that she dwells in the highest. In the first place I want you to describe what you see happening in the forum.

ORATOR: In one place I see money being counted; in another, goods being weighed. Directly across from us, oil and other things are being measured.[14]

LAYMAN: These are the works of reason,[15] by means of which men surpass the beasts. Brutes cannot number, weigh, and measure. Consider, now, and tell me, Orator, by what and in what and from what these things are done.

ORATOR: Through discretion.[16]

LAYMAN: That is correct. But how does discretion enumerate things if not by means of the *one*?[17]

ORATOR: In what way?

LAYMAN: Is not one, one times one? And two, two times one? Three, three times one? And so on?

ORATOR: Yes.

LAYMAN: All numbers are therefore produced by the one?

ORATOR: It would seem so.

LAYMAN: *One* is the principle of number; therefore, it follows that the least weight is the principle of weighing and the least measure the principle of measuring. Let the least weight be called an ounce and the least measure a foot.[18] Thus, numbering is from the one, weighing is from the ounce, and measurement is from the foot. Similarly we count in ones, weigh in ounces, and measure in feet. Is this not so?

ORATOR: It certainly is.

LAYMAN: Through what, however, is unity, the ounce, and the foot attained?

ORATOR: I do not know. I do realize that unity is not attained through number because number is posterior to one. Likewise, the ounce is not attained through weighing nor is the foot attained through measuring.

LAYMAN: You speak well, Orator. In nature the simple is prior to the composite and therefore the composite is posterior in nature. It follows that the composite cannot measure the simple, but that the reverse is true. From this, you come to understand that that by which, from which, and in which, everything that can be numbered is numbered, is not itself attainable by number. You come to realize that that by which, from which, and in which, everything that can be weighed is weighed, is not attainable by weight. Likewise, that by which, from which, and in which, every measurable thing is measured, is not attainable by measure.

ORATOR: I see this clearly.

LAYMAN: Transfer this cry of wisdom in the streets to the heights where wisdom dwells, and you will discover many things much more delightful than what is in your most adorned books.

ORATOR: I do not understand unless you explain your meaning.

LAYMAN: I am prohibited from doing this unless you ask from desire. Wisdom's secrets ought not to be revealed indiscriminately to all people.

ORATOR: I very much desire to hear you. I am excited by the little I have already heard. The things that you have previously related indicate greater things in the future. I ask you then to continue with what you have begun.

LAYMAN: I do not know if one may reveal such secrets and show that such a profundity is easy. Still, I cannot but comply with your wish. Brother, the highest wisdom is this, that you may know how in the example just given the unattainable is unattainably attained.[19]

ORATOR: You relate astonishing but incongruous things.

LAYMAN: Once such secrets are revealed they appear to be incongruous. Consequently, they should not be divulged to everyone. You are astonished that I have said something contradictory, but you will hear and taste the truth. What I have just said about unity, the ounce, and the foot, must be said about all things with respect to their first principle. For the principle of all things is that by which, in which, and from which, things with principles have principles. The principle itself, however, is not attainable by anything that has a principle. It is that by which, in which, and from which, every intelligible entity is understood. And yet it is not attainable by the intellect. Similarly, it is this principle by which, in which, and from which, all things capable of being uttered are spoken, even though the principle itself is unattainable by speech. It is likewise that by which, in which, and from which, everything capable of being limited is limited, and everything capable of having an end has an end. It cannot, however, be limited by a limit nor determined by an end. You will be able to make countless such true propositions similar to these. You can fill all the volumes of oratory, adding others to them without number, so that you may see how wisdom dwells in the highest. For the highest is that which is not able to be higher. Infinity alone is such a height. The wisdom, then, which all men seek by nature and pursue with great mental desire, is known only as being higher than all knowledge and being at the same time unknowable. It is unutterable in any language, unintelligible to every intellect, and immeasurable by every measure. It cannot be limited by any limit nor bounded by any boundary. No proportion is proportionate to it. No comparison can be compared to it, nor can it be conformed to any conformation. It cannot be formed by any formation and it cannot be moved by any motion. No imagination can imagine it, no sensation can sense it, and no attraction can attract it. It is tasteless to all tasting, inaudible to all hearing, invisible to all vision. It cannot be apprehended by any apprehension. No affirmation can affirm it, no negation can negate it, and no doubting can doubt it. It is not subject to any opinion. Because it cannot be expressed in any speech, no limit to such modes of expression can be grasped. This is because that by which, in which, and from which, all things exist is unthinkable in any thought.

ORATOR: Without a doubt these things are higher than I expected to hear. I beg you to continue leading me to where I may, along with you, so pleasantly and sweetly taste something of such high speculations. I see that you are never satiated by speaking about this wisdom. Unless you were tasting the sweetness governing this wisdom by an inner taste, I think that it would not attract you so much.

LAYMAN: Nothing tastes sweeter to the intellect than wisdom.[20] Those men who speak only by the word and not by taste ought not to be considered in any manner to be wise. Those men, however, who speak with relish about it are those who through wisdom so know all things that they know nothing at all. For all internal taste is by, from, and in that wisdom which is not able to be tasted by any taste.[21] Therefore, it is tasted untastingly because it is higher than anything that can be tasted: whether it be sensible, rational or intellectual. This is to taste untastingly and from a distance, just as a particular fragrance can be called an untastable foretaste. A fragrance given forth from a fragrant thing, received in another thing, attracts us so that we may run the course to the perfume in the fragrance of the perfumes.[22] The same thing is true with respect to eternal and infinite wisdom. Because it shines forth in all things, it attracts us by a certain foretaste of its effects so that we may be carried to it by a wonderful desire. It is the life of the spiritual intellect that has a certain connatural foretaste in itself.[23] Through this the spirit seeks the fountain of its life with great zeal.[24] It would not seek this without foretaste nor would it realize that it had received it, if indeed it did receive it. Hence, it is moved to it as to its proper life. It is sweet for every spirit continually to ascend[25] to the principle of life, even though the principle is inaccessible. To ascend to life is continually to live more happily. And when the spirit, in seeking its life, is led to the point where it sees that its life is infinite life, then the more the spirit perceives that its life is immortal, the more it rejoices.[26] Thus the inaccessibility or the incomprehensibility of the infinity of the life of the

spirit is the comprehension it most desires. It resembles someone
who may have a treasure in his life and come to realize that it is
innumerable, imponderable and immeasurable.[27] Such knowledge
of incomprehensibility is the most delightful and desired comprehension. This is because it refers not to the one comprehending,
but to the most lovable treasure of life. It is as if someone loved
something because it is lovable and rejoices that the infinite and
inexpressible cause of the love be found in the lovable object.
This is the most joyous comprehension of the lover: the comprehension of the incomprehensible lovableness of the beloved. He
would not be so delighted to love his beloved according to something comprehensible as he is when it is manifest to him that the
lovableness of his beloved is completely without measure, determination, limit, and comprehension. Such a condition is the most
joyful comprehensibility of incomprehensibility and a desirable
learned ignorance.[28] This is because the lover knows these things
in his own way and yet does not know them with precision.

ORATOR: Perhaps I understand. You must decide. For this seems
to be your meaning: our principle through which, in which, and
from which we exist and are moved is tasted by us as a principle,
a medium and an end.[29] This occurs when our principle's vital
sweetness is tasted without tasting,[30] through desire, and comprehended without comprehension, through the intellect. He who
attempts to taste it without tasting and to comprehend it without
comprehension is utterly without both taste and intellect.[31]

LAYMAN: You have grasped the principle well, Orator. Those men
who think that wisdom is nothing but what can be comprehended
by the intellect, and that happiness is nothing but what they can
obtain by themselves, are a long way from true, eternal and infinite
wisdom. They have been turned to some kind of determinable
rest[32] that they believe to be the joy of life, even though it is not.
And so, when they learn that they have been deceived, they are
in torment. Where they thought happiness was, where they turned
themselves with every effort, they will discover want and death.
Infinite wisdom, however, is the unfailing food of life. Our spirit
thrives upon it forever and is able to love nothing but wisdom
and truth. Every intellect desires being and its being is life. Its
life, however, is understanding, understanding fed by wisdom and
truth.[33] An intellect that does not taste bright wisdom is like an
eye in darkness. It is an eye, but it does not see, because it is

not in the light. It is in torment and want, in death rather than in life, because it lacks the delectable life that consists in seeing. Consequently, an intellect that is turned to anything other than to the food of eternal wisdom will discover itself to be outside of life, as if it were in the darkness of ignorance, more dead than alive.[34] The possession of intellectual being without understanding is a poverty without limit because every intellect is able to understand only through eternal wisdom.

ORATOR: You relate things that are beautiful as well as extraordinary. Please tell me how I can be raised up to some taste of eternal wisdom.

LAYMAN: Eternal wisdom is tasted in everything that is capable of being tasted. It is the delight in everything delightful. It is the beauty in everything beautiful.[35] It is the thing longed for in every longing. And so on for all the things that are desirable. How can it then not be tasted? Is your life not pleasing to you when it goes according to your desire?

ORATOR: Yes, exactly!

LAYMAN: In every desire of intellectual life you desire nothing more than the eternal wisdom that is the complement, principle, medium and end of your desire. This is because your desire does not exist except through the eternal wisdom from which and in which it has being. Similarly, this happy life that you desire would not exist except in the same eternal wisdom in which it has existence and outside of which it is not able to exist. Therefore, if this desire for immortal life, to live in eternal happiness, is sweet to you, then you are experiencing in yourself a certain foretaste of eternal wisdom. This is because nothing utterly unknown is desired. There are apples in India that we do not desire because we have no foretaste of them. Because we cannot love without nourishment, we desire it and have a certain foretaste of it in order that we may live through the senses. Thus the child has a certain foretaste of milk in his nature. When he is hungry he is moved to seek milk, for we are nourished by those things that sustain our existence. In the same way the intellect has its life from eternal wisdom, and it has some foretaste of this. In all the food that the intellect requires in order to live, it is moved only toward that food that provides it with its intellectual being. If, therefore, in every desire of intellectual life you would attend to that by which the intellect exists, and through which and to which it is moved, you would discover in

yourself that the sweetness of eternal wisdom is that which makes
your desire so sweet and delightful for you. And so you are
carried by an inexpressible desire to its comprehension as to the
immortality of your life. Consider iron and the magnet. Iron has
the principle of its effluence in the magnet. And when the presence
of the magnet excites the heavy iron, it is moved by a wonderful
desire that goes beyond the motion of nature.[36] Because of its
weight the iron ought to tend downwards. It is moved upwards,
however, by uniting itself to its principle. Were there no natural
foretaste in the iron for the magnet, it no more would be moved
to the magnet than to another stone. Such attraction would not
exist unless there were in the magnet a greater inclination to iron
than to copper. Therefore, our intellectual spirit has a principle
of intellectual being from eternal wisdom in such a manner that
its being is more conformed to wisdom than to some other non-
intellectual being. Hence the illumination or inspiration of the
holy soul is a desirable motion with respect to the stimulation of
the soul.[37] For he who seeks wisdom by intellectual movement is
inwardly transported to the foretasted sweetness where he forgets
himself. The sweetness is received by the body as if it were from
outside the body.[38] The weight of nothing sensible can restrain
him from uniting himself to the attracting wisdom. Abandoning
the faculty of sense out of any amazed[39] admiration that causes the
soul to become senseless, he comes to regard everything except
wisdom as being utterly nothing. To such men it is sweet to be
able to relinquish this world and this life in order to be transported
more easily into the wisdom of immortality. This foretaste turns
all things that appear to be delightful into an abomination to holy
men, who endure all corporeal pain with an even spirit so as to
attain wisdom more quickly. It teaches us that our spirit can
never fail once it has turned to wisdom. If our body can never
hold the spirit by means of any sensible binding, then the spirit
can never fail because of a failing body when it has dismissed its
corporeal office in order to be borne most eagerly to wisdom. This
assimilation is in our spirit by its nature and it cannot come to a
state of repose except in wisdom. Our spirit is as it were a living
image of wisdom. The image, however, is not at rest except
in what it is the image of and from which it has its principle,
medium and end. The living image exhibits by its life a motion
away from its own self toward the exemplar in which it alone

comes to rest. For the life of the image cannot come to rest in its own self because it is the life of the life of truth and not its own. And so it is moved to its exemplar as to the truth of its being. If the exemplar is eternal, and the image has its life in which it experiences a foretaste of its exemplar, then it is moved to it by desire. Because such vital motion cannot come to rest in anything other than in the infinite life that is eternal wisdom, vital spiritual motion cannot cease. Even in infinity it never attains infinite life, but is always moved by the most joyful desire. In this way it attains that which is never rejected. This is because of the delightfulness of the attraction.[40] Wisdom is the most savoury food which, in satisfying, does not diminish the desire to partake of it. Thus the delight of the eternal banquet never ceases.

ORATOR: I clearly see that which you have so well explained. Yet I see that there is much to explain about the taste of wisdom on the one hand and about what can be revealed concerning taste on the other.

LAYMAN: Well said. It pleases me to have heard you say that. Just as all wisdom about the taste of a thing that has never been tasted is empty and sterile, until it is tasted, so it is with this wisdom. No one tastes it through hearing, but only he who receives it by an internal tasting. Such a person gives testimony, not about what he has heard, but about what he has tasted in himself by experience.[41] Knowledge of the many descriptions of love that the saints have left us, without tasting of the love, is a kind of emptiness. Wherefore, it is not sufficient for one seeking eternal wisdom to know those things that are written about it. It is necessary that he make it his own when he discovers by his intellect where it is. He is like the man who discovers a field in which there is a treasure. He cannot rejoice about the treasure as long as it is in someone else's field and not in his own. So he sells everything and buys that field so that he may have the treasure in a field that belongs to him.[42] But he must sell and give away all of his own things because eternal wisdom will not be possessed except where one has kept nothing of one's own for the sake of possessing it. Those things that belong to us are the vices; from eternal wisdom comes nothing but good. Thus the spirit of wisdom does not dwell in a body subject to sins nor in a malevolent soul.[43] It dwells rather in its own pure field and in the clear image of wisdom as if in its own holy temple. Eternal wisdom resides where the Lord's field is, bearing immortal fruit. This is the field of the virtues which wisdom cultivates and where the fruits of the spirit grow. They are justice, peace, fortitude, temperance, chastity, patience, and the like.[44]

ORATOR: You have explained these things fully. But tell me now whether God is not the principle of all things.

LAYMAN: Who doubts that?

ORATOR: Is eternal wisdom anything other than God?

LAYMAN: It can be nothing else but God.

ORATOR: Has God not formed all things through the Word?[45]

LAYMAN: He has.

ORATOR: Is the Word God?[46]

LAYMAN: It is.

ORATOR: Is it also wisdom?

LAYMAN: To say that God made all things in wisdom is no different from saying that He created all things in the Word.[47] Consider how everything that exists has been able to exist and that it has been able to exist in a definite manner and does so exist. God, who transmits the actuality of existing, exists. With Him is the omnipotence by which a thing can be brought forth into being from non-being. He is also God the Father, who can be called unity or entity,[48] because He necessitates from His omnipotence the being that was nothing. In fact, God transmits a specific sort of being to a creature so that it exists as the heavens, for example, and as nothing else, neither more nor less.[49] And this God is the Word, Wisdom or the Son of the Father. He may be called the equality of unity or of entity. Next there is being so united as to exist. And it has this from God who is the connection that unites all things. This is God the Holy Spirit; He unites and binds together all things in us and in the universe. As nothing begets the unity that is the first principle without beginning,[50] so nothing begets the Father who is eternal. Equality, however, proceeds from units and its equality.[51] Because of this, everything requires the triune principle in order not only to have being but the particular being that a thing has.[52] This principle is God, the three and the one. It might be possible to say more about this if time permitted.

Wisdom, which is therefore the equality of being, is the Word or the reason of things. It is, as it were, the infinite intellectual form; the form that gives formed being to a thing. Accordingly, the infinite form is the actuality of all forms that may be formed and is the most precise equality of all such things. The infinite circle, if it were to exist, would be the true exemplar of all figures that can be drawn and the equality of the being of every figure. It would be a triangle, a hexagon, a decagon and so forth. Although it is the simplest figure, it is the most adequate measure of all figures. Likewise, infinite wisdom is a simplicity enfolding[53] all forms, of which it is the most adequate measure. It is as if art itself, in the most perfect idea of omnipotent art, were to be everything formable through art by the most simple form. If you consider the human form, you discover that the form of the divine art is its most precise exemplar. It is as if there were nothing else than the exemplar of the human form. This being so, if you consider the form of the heavens and attend to the form of the divine art, you will be completely unable to conceive of it as anything other than the exemplar of this form of the heavens. The same is true for all forms either formed already or capable of being formed. Thus the art or wisdom of God the Father is the most simple form. Yet it is the single most equal exemplar of all the infinite forms that can be formed, even though they are of variable things.

How wonderful is such a form! None of the forms that are capable of being formed are able to unfold[54] this most simple infinity. He alone who raises himself above all opposition by the highest intellect sees that this alone is most true. Were he to attend to the natural power that is in unity and were he to conceive of it as being in act as a certain formal being that is visible to the intellect alone, but from afar, he would see it. Because the power of unity would be the most simple power, it would be a certain most simple infinity. Next, if he attended to the form of numbers, considering either twos or tens, and then returned to the actual force of unity, he would see that form which is posited as being the actual power of unity. It is the most precise exemplar of duality and likewise for tenness and for all other denumerable numbers. The infinity of that form that is called the power of unity would produce this result: while you consider duality, that form cannot be either greater or less than the form of duality of which it is the most precise exemplar. And so you see that the unique and simplest wisdom of God is the truest exemplar of every form that can be formed, because it is infinite. And this is His touching, by means of which He touches all things, limiting them and setting them in order. He is in all the forms as truth is in an image, an exemplar in a copy, a form in a figure, and precision in its assimilation. And even though He communicates Himself most liberally to all things, because He is the infinite good, nonetheless He cannot be grasped in anything as He is. Infinite identity cannot be received in another thing, because it would be received in another in a different manner. Although it is not able to be received in another except in a different manner, it is still received in the better mode. An infinity that cannot be multiplied is unfolded better in a differentiated reception. For great diversity expresses better that which cannot be multiplied. And so it happens that when wisdom is received in various forms in different ways, everything called to identity participates in wisdom in the manner appropriate to each thing. As some things participate in wisdom in a spirit quite distant from the first form, it scarcely assigns elemental being to them. It assigns mineral being to those that are formed in a more complete degree while it confers vegetative life to those of a nobler degree. To others still higher it gives sensibility. After this it assigns imagination, reason, and finally intellect. Intellect is the highest degree, namely the closest image of wisdom. It alone is the degree that has the aptitude to raise itself up to the taste of wisdom. This is because the image of wisdom in such intellectual natures is the living mode of life for intellectual being. The power of this mode of life is the exertion of a vital motion from itself that proceeds through intellection to its proper object, which is absolute truth—eternal wisdom. Because this procession is intellection, it is also an intellectual tasting. Apprehension through the intellect is an attainment of a quiddity by a most pleasing tasting to the extent that it is able to apprehend it. A certain pleasing sweetness of the quiddity is perceived in external things through sensation by sensible tasting. This does not attain the quiddity of a thing. Intellectual sweetness, which is the image of the sweetness of eternal wisdom, the quiddity of quiddities, is tasted in the quiddity by the intellect. It is a disproportionate comparison of one sweetness to another.

Let these things that have been said suffice for the moment to reveal to you that wisdom is not in the art of oratory or in great volumes. Rather it is found in a separation from such sensible things, and by a conversion to a most simple and infinite form. It is received in a temple that is purged of all vice by a fervent love in which you must abide until you may be able to taste it and learn how sweet that is which is the sweetness of all things. Once you have tasted it, all of the things that now seem great to you will become vile. You will be humbled so that nothing of arrogance or of any other vice may remain in you. This is because once you have tasted wisdom you will adhere to it inseparably with a chaste and pure heart. You will desert the world and the things that are not wisdom for wisdom's sake. Living with indescribable gladness, you will die and rest eternally after death in this wisdom's most loving embrace. May the ever blessed wisdom of God concede this to both of us. Amen.

END OF THE FIRST BOOK OF THE LAYMAN

NOTES

1   Notice the contrasts: pride (*fastus*) versus humility (*humilitas*) and knowledge (*scientia*) versus foolishness (*stultitia*).

2   I Cor. 3:19 and I Cor. 8:1. Notice that "knowledge of this world" is contrasted with "true knowledge." The layman makes it clear that he is not anti-intellectual. N. B. All Scriptural references are based on the Latin *Vulgate*.

3   Notice the contrast between gladness (*laetitia*) and the implied deadly sin of sadness (*tristitia*).

4   *Studium litterarum.*

5   The *locus classicus* for discussions of rhetorical method during the Renaissance was Plato, *Phaedrus* 275C–D. Cusanus owned a copy of this dialogue; Cf. *Cusanus Codex* 177.16. Cf. N. W. Gilbert, *Renaissance Concepts of Method* (New York, 1963) 3.

6   Psalms 123:7.

7   *Phaedrus* 248B-C. Cf. *Protagoras* 313C–314.

8   Ephesians 4:13. "Perfection" is commonly regarded as the last stage of the mystical way. Cusanus will also refer to it as "rest" at other places in the dialogue. In the Middle Ages, perfection was regarded as the state in which the creature came to rest according to its nature.

9   *Additamenta.* Literally, "things added on," i.e., the store of wisdom compiled from the different *auctores*. Cf. Fr. E. A. Quain, "The Medieval Accessus ad auctores," *Traditio* III (1945) 215-64.

10   Proverbs 1:20; Ecclesiasticus 24:7.

11   Nicholas of Cusa, *Apologia doctae ignorantiae.* This work represents Cusanus' attempt to explicate the concept of *ignorantia scientia.*

12   For the symbolism of the book of nature in medieval literature, cf. E. R. Curtius' *European Literature and the Latin Middle Ages* (New York, 1963), ch. 16, sec. 7. To this standard motif, Cusanus adds a distinction in the *Layman* between an external book of nature that constitutes the sensible world and the internal book of nature that is the human mind. He may have discovered this distinction in St. Bonaventure's *Breviloquium* II.11.2.

13   Luke 11:20.

14   Wisdom 11:21; Job 28:25. Notice that counting, weighing and measuring employ arithmetic, the first of the quadrivial sciences. This is in seeming contrast to the trivial arts of the orator: grammar, rhetoric and dialectic.

15   *Ratio.* This term can refer to a calculation in arithmetic as well as to the faculty of reason. The layman's point employs both senses.

16   *Discretio.* In late medieval Latin this term can refer to the faculty of making distinctions as well as to the distinctions themselves as independent logical entities. The faculty is best rendered as *discretion*.

17   Plato, *Parmenides* 137C–142 and 143C–144B. For a discussion of the

causal power of the one, cf. Cusanus' *De visione Dei*, ch. 17. Cusanus' analysis had a great influence on Neoplatonic metaphysics in the Renaissance. Cf. Giordano Bruno *De la causa, principio e uno*, dialogues 4 and 5; Pico della Mirandola, *De ente et uno*. Marsilio Ficino discusses the doctrine in many places in his writings.

18 *Unica*. This term implies a simple unit. *Petitum* is derived from the Greek word for foot. In Latin it is *pes*.

19 As the remainder of this dialogue will reveal, the precise wording of this somewhat awkward passage is important.

20 Cusanus is playing on the Latin term *sapere*. It can indicate the act of tasting or the state of being wise. Thus in English "sapient" means wise and "saporous" means tasty.

21 Romans 11:36. The phrasing "by, in, and from" was used by the medieval scholastics to refer to the identification of the agent, formal, and final cause of the universe with the second person of the Trinity. It is this sense that Cusanus is employing here. It is therefore no surprise when he later identifies wisdom with the Word.

22 Song of Songs 1:3.

23 This reading is preferred to "The life itself is a . . ." mainly because it makes more sense. It also seems to be more consistent with another passage found in Cusanus *De dato patris luminum* (Heidelberg, 1937) IV, 67. The Latin formulae are almost identical, but the *De dato* passage is not ambiguous. The term *spiritus intellectualis* is found in three manuscripts.

24 Psalms 35:10; Proverbs 14:27.

25 *Ascendere*. Cusanus is referring to the Neoplatonic doctrine that the soul has a natural tendency to ascend to its source or principle.

26 The ascent of the soul is conditioned by an inner perception. Cf. n. 12. Cusanus seems to be referring to the mystical doctrine of illumination. Cf. M. L. Führer, "Purgation, Illumination and Perfection in Nicholas of Cusa," *Downside Review* 98 (1980) 169–189.

27 Wisdom 7:14. Cf. Matthew 6:21 and Luke 13:44.

28 Cusanus' first major philosophical treatise was *On Learned Ignorance*.

29 Cusanus seems to follow Ulrich of Strasbourg (*De summo bono*, Bk II, Tract. v) in using these scholastic terms as follows:

principle	agent cause	"from which"
medium	formal cause	"by which"
end	final cause	"in which"

Scholastics seem to have agreed that the agent cause was the first principle or source of motion, the formal cause was that which determined the matter of a thing and the final cause was the purpose of an action.

30 *Ingustabiliter gustatur*.

31 Cusanus seems to mean that these faculties have been transcended.

32 The determinable rest of a motion would correspond to its final cause.

33 Cf. Proclus, *The Elements of Theology*, ed. E. R. Dodds (Oxford, 1964).

34 Plato, *Sophist* 254A. Cf. Ps-Dionysius, *On the Divine Names* IV, 5 (PG III, 701).

35 Plato, *Phaedo* 100D.

36 *Supra motum naturae*. This phrase seems to express a Thomistic-like theory of grace that perfects nature without destroying it. At any rate, Cusanus is suggesting an analogy to the transcendence of the spiritual life that he will develop throughout the rest of the first book of *The Layman*.

37 Proclus, *op.cit.*, props. 64 and 71.

38 This passage is obscure. A mystical construction may be intended, but the sense is not clear.

39 *Stupida*. This term can also mean "stupid" or "senseless." It is related to the term *"idiota"* in the sense that one who has transcended the senses in the admiration for the divine would appear to be a "senseless idiot." For an analysis of the Platonic source for this doctrine see Josef Pieper, *Enthusiasm and Divine Madness* (New York, 1964), ch. 5.

40 Reading *attractus* instead of *attactus*.

41 Oratorical learning lacks the dimension of experience and is thus empty and sterile. Inner experience is emphasized by the *via moderna*. Elisabeth Bohnenstädt suggests that this passage reflects the influence of Jan van Ruysbroeck. Cf. *Der Laie über die Weisheit*, ed. E. Bohnenstädt (Leipzig, 1944) 97–98.

42 Matthew 13:14. Cf. Cusanus, *De visione Dei*, ch. 16, for an analysis of the theme of wisdom as a treasure.

43 This passage is taken almost verbatim from Wisdom 1:4.

44 Cusanus appears to have Galatians 5:22 in mind. He adds three of the four cardinal virtues; this suggests that he was thinking of the mystical doctrine of the infused virtues.

45 Wisdom 9:1.

46 John 1:1.

47 Psalms 32:6; 103:24.

48 *Entitas*. As Cusanus uses it throughout his writings, this terms denotes a more abstract concept of being than *esse*. Cusanus may have intended John Scotus Erigena's distinction between creating being (*entitas*) and created being (*esse*).

49 Plato, *Philebus* 24A; Aristotle, *Physics* 219B.

50 Another reading could be, "the first principle without principle." It would be similar to the scholastic formula, "the first mover unmoved" as a name for God in the order of efficient causality.

51 *Codex Chicaginensis* n. 37571 adds: "And thus the Holy Spirit proceeds from the Father and the Son."

52 Et tale esse, in quo est.

53 *Complicans*. Cusanus gives this term, along with its counterpart *"expli-*

cans," a special Neoplatonic meaning. The "enfolding" of creation is the Christian version of the return of all creatures to the One. Because it is part of the *opus restaurationis* (the work of redemption), Cusanus identifies it with the wisdom that is the Word. The "unfolding" is the cosmic theophany of the Trinity. Cf. E. Vansteenberghe, *Le Cardinal Nicolas de Cues* (Paris, 1920) 310–312.

54 *Explicare*. Cf. n. 53.

BOOK II

The Layman on Wisdom

It happened that the Roman Orator was suspended[1] in the highest admiration after he had heard the words of the Layman about wisdom. Finding the Layman secluded in the vicinity of the Temple of Eternity,[2] he addressed him as follows:

ORATOR: You are the man whom I most desire to see.[3] Help my inability so that I may feed with some facility upon the difficult things that transcend my mind. Otherwise it will be of little profit to have heard so many profound theories[4] from you.

LAYMAN: There is no difficulty easier to contemplate than to contemplate divine things. Here difficulty coincides with delight. Tell me, however, what it is that you desire?

ORATOR: Tell me how I can form a concept of a God who is greater than can be conceived?[5]

LAYMAN: Do it in the same way that you would with a concept.

ORATOR: Explain, please.

LAYMAN: You have heard how the inconceivable is conceived in every concept. Consequently, a concept of a concept approaches the inconceivable.

ORATOR: How may I form a more precise concept?

LAYMAN: Think of precision, for God is absolute precision itself.[6]

ORATOR: What should I do then when I propose to form a correct concept of God?

LAYMAN: Contemplate truth itself.

ORATOR: What if I propose to form a just concept?

LAYMAN: Turn to justice.

ORATOR: And when I seek to attain a good concept of God, what shall I do?

LAYMAN: Raise the mind's eye to goodness.[7]

ORATOR: I wonder where you are sending me in all of these things.

LAYMAN: See how easy the difficulty is in divine things: it always offers itself to the one seeking it according to the way in which it is sought.

ORATOR: Without a doubt, nothing is more wonderful.

LAYMAN: Every question about God presupposes the thing questioned.[8] And the reply must be what is presupposed in any question about God because He is signified in every signification of terms, even though He Himself is unsignifiable.

ORATOR: Please explain. I am so amazed that I scarcely hear what you are saying.

LAYMAN: Does not the question whether something exists presuppose entity?

ORATOR: Yes, indeed.

LAYMAN: Therefore, when you are asked about God's existence, answer by means of that which is presupposed. That is, reply that He does exist because He is the entity presupposed by the question. So, if anyone should ask *what* God is, answer that God is absolute quiddity,[9] because the question presupposes that quiddity exists. And so it is for all things. Nor is it suitable to doubt this. God is the absolute presupposition of all the things that are presupposed in any way, just as a cause is presupposed in every effect. See then, Orator, how easy theological difficulty is.

ORATOR: Certainly such facility is very great and amazing.

LAYMAN: I tell you that God is infinite facility itself. It does not suit God that He should be infinite difficulty. It is necessary, as you will soon learn concerning the curved and the straight, that difficulty pass over into facility if it is to apply to the infinite God.

ORATOR: If that which is presupposed in any question is the solution of a question in theological matters, then there is no question proper to God because the answer coincides with it.[10]

LAYMAN: Your inference is good. But add that, because of God's infinite rectitude and absolute necessity, a doubtful question does not touch Him; all doubt is certainty in God. Thus no answer to a question about God is proper and precise, because precision is one and infinite, which is God. In fact every reply participates in the absolute reply, which is infinitely precise. But that which I told you concerning the way in which the presupposed is the response to theological questions must be understood according to the mode in which the question exists. Were you to grasp it this way, it would be sufficient because neither a question nor the rejoinder to a question concerning God can attain precision. Thus the response to the presupposed is in the manner in which the question approaches precision. This is our sufficiency that we have from God: the knowledge that we are not able to attain unattainable precision except by some manner of participation in the mode of absolute precision. Among the various and many modes that participate at the same time in the one mode of precision, the mode we just spoke about approaches nearest to absolute facility. It is our sufficiency because we cannot attain any other that would at the same time be easier or truer.

ORATOR: Who would not be astonished upon hearing these things? Because God is absolute incomprehensibility, you say that comprehension approaches Him more closely the more its mode participates in facility.

LAYMAN: He who sees[11] with me that absolute facility coincides with absolute incomprehensibility is not able to affirm it except as I do. I thus constantly affirm that insofar as the universal mode was easier with respect to any questions that can be formed about God, it is truer and more appropriate insofar as positive affirmation is appropriate to God.

ORATOR: Please explain this.

LAYMAN: This pertains to our admission that something can be said affirmatively about God. In that theology, however, which negates all things about God, we ought to speak otherwise, because in such a theology the truer reaction is a negation to every question. But in that mode we are not led to the knowledge of what God is, only to what He is not. Since neither affirmation nor negation is appropriate to God, inasmuch as He is beyond every affirmation and negation, there is a consideration of God in which the reply is the negation of affirmation, negation, and conjunction. According to affirmation, when it is asked whether God exists, the response must come from the presupposition that He does exist and that this existence is the presupposed absolute entity. According to negation, the truer response must be that He does not exist because none of all the things that can be said according to this way of speaking of the ineffable would be appropriate. But consistent with the way of speaking that is above every affirmation and negation, the rejoinder must be that He neither is nor is not absolute entity, nor both together, but that He is beyond them. Now I think that you understand what I mean.

ORATOR: I understand now that you want to say that in that theological discourse, where we allow expressions about God and where the power of a word is not completely reduced, you have restored the sufficiency of difficult things to the facility of the mode of forming truer propositions about God.

LAYMAN: You have understood well. If I have to reveal to you the concept of God that I have, it is necessary that my speech be of significant language so that I might be of service to you in leading you to what is sought by its power, which is commonly known by us. God, however, is what is sought. This is theological discourse, therefore, in which I strive to lead you to God through the power of language and in a way that is easier and truer for my ability.

ORATOR: Please allow us to return now to those things that were touched on before and explain them in their order. In the beginning you said that the concept of a concept is a concept of God because God is the concept of a concept.[12] Is it not the mind that conceives?

LAYMAN: Without the mind there is no concept.[13]

ORATOR: Since conception belongs to the mind, the conception of an absolute concept is nothing but the conception of the art of the absolute mind.

LAYMAN: Continue, you are on the right path.

ORATOR: The art of the absolute mind is nothing other than the form of all things that can be formed. So I see how the concept of a concept is nothing but the concept of an idea of the divine art. Tell me if what I say is true.

LAYMAN: Very much so. Indeed, the absolute concept cannot be anything other than the ideal form of all the things that can be conceived. It is the equality of all the things that can be formed.

ORATOR: This concept is called, I believe, the Word or the Reason of God.[14]

LAYMAN: No matter how it is referred to by the learned, all things are in that concept. It is similar to our saying that those things that do not come forth into being without a prior reason exist antecedently in reason. All of the things, however, that we see existing, have a reason for their being. Thus, they exist according to the mode in which they exist and in no other. Therefore, he who looks with a profound mind into the simplicity of absolute reason, which, by way of priority, enfolds all things in itself, produces a concept about the absolute concept or about the concept *per se*. This is what I postulated in the beginning.

ORATOR: Enough about this. Now show how the concept of absolute precision is a more precise concept of God.

LAYMAN: I do not have the time to repeat the same thing in its particulars, neither do I see that it is necessary for you because access to all things is open to you from one thing. Accept, then, an answer in the briefest form possible. Precision, rectitude,[15] truth, justice, and goodness, about which you have heard, are the same thing. Do not think that I wish to speak according to the mode in which all of theology is placed in a circle so that one attribute is verified of another. For that would be to claim by means of the necessity of the infinity of God's simplicity that God's magnitude is God's potency and the converse, that the potency of God is the power of God,[16] and so on, for all that we attribute to the essence of God. We experience these things about which we are now conversing as coinciding in our common discourse. Upon hearing someone describe a thing as it is, one person says that he described it precisely, another that he described it correctly, another that he described it truly, another that he expressed it justly, and another that he expressed it well. We definitely find it to be so in our daily speech. He who says that someone spoke precisely or correctly, wishes to say only that he spoke justly or well. And you discover this to be true for yourself when you see how someone who said neither more nor less than he ought to say, attained all these things. Precision is truly nothing but what is neither more nor less. In the same way neither the correct, the true, the just, nor the good admit of either more or less. Indeed, how could anything be precise, correct, true, just, or even good when it is less than precise, correct, true, just, and good? And if that which is less than precise, correct, true, just, and good is not precise, correct, true, just, and good, it is clear how that which admits of more is none of these things. For a precision that admits of more, that is, that can be more precise, is not absolute precision. The same applies to the correct, the true, the just, and the good.

ORATOR: There is then no concept of God formed through those things that admit of a more or a less.

LAYMAN: Your inference is very good. Because God is infinite, those things that admit of a more or a less are less assimilated to Him. Therefore, in those things one neither ascends nor descends into infinity, as we experience in number and in the division of a continuum.

ORATOR: There is, therefore, no precision in this world. Nor is there rectitude, truth, justice, or goodness because we experience one thing to be more precise than another, as one picture is more precise than another. The same holds true for rectitude; one thing is more correct, more true, more just or better than another.

LAYMAN: You understand well. Those things, when they have been freed from the more and the less, are not of this world. For nothing is found to be so precise that it is not able to be more precise, correct, true, just, or better. And so the precision, rectitude, truth, justice, or goodness found in this world are participants in such absolutes and are the images of which these are the exemplars. I speak of exemplars in the plural when reference is made to the various reasons for the various things; in truth, however, there is but one exemplar because these others coincide in the absolute.

ORATOR: I very much desire to hear from you how there is but one exemplar for such a great variety of universals.

LAYMAN: He who is little versed in such theological speculations believes this to be very difficult.[17] To me, however, nothing seems to be easier and more delightful. The absolute exemplar, which is nothing but absolute precision, rectitude, truth, justice, or goodness, enfolds all the things that can be exemplified.[18] It is indeed a more perfect precision, rectitude, truth, justice, and goodness of all such things than is your face for all the images that can be formed of it and of which it is the precision, rectitude, and truth.[19] All of the images that may be formed of your face are precise, correct, and true insofar as they partake of and imitate the image of your living face. Although it is not possible for one image to be depicted as being another without differences, because precision is not of this world and that which is another thing must exist in another mode, nevertheless, there is but one exemplar for all of this variety.

ORATOR: What you say about the unity of the exemplar is true, but not with respect to equality. Although my face is the measure of the truth of the paintings, because the image is judged by seeing the face as being either more or less lacking in the depiction, yet it is not true that my face is the most adequate measure of all things by every mode of measure. This is because it is always either a more or a less.

LAYMAN: What you say about your face is true. Being a quantity and of a nature that receives a more and a less, it can be neither precision nor an adequate measure of another thing. In a world lacking precision, an adequate measure or similitude is not possible. So if you conceive of an absolute exemplar it must be otherwise, because it is neither great nor small. Such things are not able to exist with respect to the reason of the exemplar. An ant, when it is painted, is no less an exemplar than a painted mountain and vice versa. Therefore, the absolute exemplar, which receives neither a more nor a less because it is precision and truth, cannot be more or less than the exemplified. For that which cannot be less we call the minimum; it is little in the greatest degree. That which cannot be greater, we call the maximum; it is great in the greatest degree. Absolve greatness[20] from that which is little and that which is great in the greatest degree. You may then see greatness in itself, not contracted in the small or the great.[21] You will see absolute greatness. It is therefore prior to the great and the small so that it cannot be greater or smaller. It is the maximum in which the minimum coincides. Therefore, such a maximum as is the absolute exemplar cannot be more or less than any admissible exemplification. That, however, which is neither more nor less, we call equal. The absolute exemplar,[22] therefore, is equality, precision, measure, or justice. It is the same thing as truth and goodness. It is the perfection of everything exemplified.

ORATOR: Please teach me also how infinity agrees with absolute rectitude.

LAYMAN: Gladly! You know that the greater a circle is, the greater its diameter is.

ORATOR: I admit that I do.

LAYMAN: Although a circle that admits of a more and a less cannot simply be the maximum or the infinite circle, let us nevertheless conceive of a circle being infinite. Will its diameter not be an infinite line?

ORATOR: By necessity it must.

LAYMAN: And the circumference, when it is infinite, will be the diameter. This is because there cannot be two infinites; one of them could always become greater by the addition of the other. And the circumference itself would not be able to be curved. It would be impossible for it to be either greater or less than the diameter if it were curved. The reason for this is that there is but one relation[23] of all circles of curved circumferences of a diameter to the circumference, which is a relation of more than three. Therefore, if the circumference is equal to the diameter, it will itself be the diameter and thus a straight line.[24] For this reason you see how the arc of a great circle bears a greater similitude to a straight line than to the arc of a little circle. From this it follows that the circumference of an infinite circle would be straight. It is then manifest to you that curvature that admits of a more and a less is not found in the infinite where there is only straightness.[25]

ORATOR: What you say certainly pleases me because it raises me easily to what is sought. Proceed please to the explanation of how infinite rectitude would be an exemplar.

LAYMAN: You most clearly perceive by yourself that infinite rectitude is related to all things as the infinite line, were it to exist, would be to figures.[26] For if infinite rectitude, which is necessarily absolute, were contracted to a line, it would by necessity be discerned as the enfolding, precision, rectitude, truth, measure, and perfection of all figures that can be drawn. Absolute rectitude, considered as absolutely and completely uncontracted to a line or to anything else, is likewise the absolute exemplar, precision, truth, measure, and perfection of all things.

ORATOR: These things cannot be doubted. But show how an infinite line is the precision of all figures. You said previously that an infinite circle is the exemplar of all figures, but I did not understand you. I have now come to you because I wish to be more clearly informed about this matter. Now you say that an infinite line is a precision; something I do not comprehend too well.

LAYMAN: You have heard how an infinite line is a circle. In the same way it is a triangle, a quadrangle, a pentagon; indeed, every infinite figure coincides with an infinite line. Hence an infinite line is an exemplar of all the figures that can be constructed from lines, because an infinite line is the infinite act or form of all the figures that can be formed. When you have studied a triangle and raised yourself up to the infinite line, you will discover that it is the most adequate exemplar of this triangle. Consider the infinite triangle. It is neither more nor less than the one designated, because the sides of an infinite triangle are infinite.[27] An infinite side, however, because it is the maximum in which the minimum coincides, is neither more nor less than the stipulated side. Thus the sides of an infinite triangle are neither more nor less than the one stipulated. An infinite triangle, therefore, is the precision and the absolute form of the finite triangle. The three sides of an infinite triangle, however, must be one infinite line because a plurality of infinite lines is not possible. It would follow, then, that an infinite line is the most precise exemplar of a given triangle. And what I have said about the triangle applies in the same way to all figures.

ORATOR: O wonderful facility of difficulties. I see now that all of these things most clearly follow from the affirmation of an infinite line. It is the exemplar, precision, correctness, truth, measure or justice, goodness or perfection of all figures that can be constructed by means of the line. And I perceive that in the simplicity of its rectitude all the things that can be constructed exist truly, formally, precisely, free from all confusion and defect because they are enfolded in the infinite that is more perfect than can be constructed.

LAYMAN: Blessed be God, who has used me, a most ignorant man, as a kind of instrument to open the eyes of your mind so that you may behold Him with a wonderful facility in the mode by which He has made Himself visible to you. For when you pass from rectitude contracted to a line to absolute infinite rectitude, you will discover in this rectitude the enfolding of everything that can be formed and the species of all things, as I have postulated with respect to figures. You will discover also how rectitude itself is the exemplar, precision, truth, measure, or justice, goodness or perfection of all the things that exist or are able to exist. It is the precise and unconfused actuality of all existing or producible things. So, to whatever species or being you turn your eyes, if you raise your mind up to infinite rectitude, you will find it to be the most precise exemplary truth of it, without defect. When, for example, you see a man who is a right and true man, he is nothing but that rectitude, truth, measure, and perfection so contracted as to terminate in a man. Were you to consider his rectitude, which is finite, and raise yourself to infinite rectitude, you would immediately see how absolute and infinite rectitude cannot be more or less than that rectitude contracted in a man by means of which he is a right and true man. His precision is the truest, the justest, and the best. Thus, infinite truth is the precision of finite truth and the infinite is the absolute precision, measure, truth, and perfection of everything finite. And you may understand all things in the same way that we have spoken about man. So now you have that which is allowed for contemplation in eternal wisdom in order that you may see all things in a most simple rectitude, most truly, most precisely, without confusion, and most perfectly, even though the vision of God is not possible in this world except in an enigmatic manner. This is true until such time as God grants that He be made visible to us without enigma. This then is the facility of the difficult things of wisdom which, because of your desire and devotion, I pray that God may daily make clearer to both of us until He bears us to the glorious fruition of truth, where we shall forever remain. Amen.

END OF THE SECOND BOOK OF THE LAYMAN

NOTES

1 *In summa admiratione suspensum. Suspensus* can mean either "suspended," "anxious," or "doubtful." St. Bonaventure uses the term in the prologue to his *Itinerarium mentis in Deum* to indicate the stage that the soul must go through in order to pass over into wisdom.

2 Although Pauly-Wissowa, *Real-Encyklopädie*, does not list anything on a Temple of Eternity in Rome, it does mention a temple dedicated to "Roma Aeterna et Venus Felix." This temple was built by Hadrian and Antonius Pius. It may be the temple that Cusanus wishes to identify.

3 This is actually a vocative.

4 The term "theory" has a theological connotation that Cusanus refers to in his treatise *De apice theoriae*. In the *De quaerendo Deum* Cusanus claims that "theory" is a composite of the terms "to see," "to run," and "God." Thus "theory" means "to run to see God."

5 "God is that in respect to which a greater cannot be conceived." This formula can be traced to St. Anselm of Canterbury.

6 *De docta ignorantia* II, 1 (Heidelberg ed.) I, p. 62. Cf. *De mente*, ch. 7.

7 *Oculi mentis.* Cf. Hugh of St. Victor, *De sacramentis* I, x, 2 (PL 176, 329C–330A).

8 *De docta ig.* I, 21, p. 44; II, 3, p. 72.

9 Cusanus is intent upon moving from a question (*quid est*) to the essence or whatness (*quidditas*) presupposed. The presupposition is more apparent in Latin.

10 The orator is asserting that for a question to be appropriate its answer must not coincide with it.

11 *Intuetur.* This term implies a direct, non-deductive, non-discursive understanding.

12 Conception is understood to be not only in the order of the mind but also in the order of generation.

13 *De mente*, ch. 8.

14 The *logos* of St. John's Gospel would ordinarily be translated into medieval Latin indifferently as *verbum* or *ratio*.

15 *Rectitudo.* This term can be translated as correctness or straightness. The Layman will later refer to truth as rectitude or correctness.

16 *Virtus* means power. The terms differs from potency (*potentia*) in that it is active and in the realm of the actual while potency is only in the realm of possibility.

17 *De mente*, ch. 3.

18 *De docta ig.* II, 3 & 7, pp. 69 & 81.

19 *De mente*, ch. 9.

20 *Maximitas.*

21 *Contractio.* Cusanus defines contraction as the principle that restricts an exemplar to some particular identity according to the proper nature of

the particular individual. Thus a multiplicity of exemplars is merely a *distinctio mentis* for Cusanus. Cf. *De docta ig.* II, 4.

22 *De docta ig.* II, 11, p. 99.

23 *Habitudo* can mean a habit, a relation, or a condition.

24 *Rectus* can mean "straight" if predicated of a geometrical object, "correct" if predicated of anything else, e.g., a concept or a person.

25 *De docta ig.* I, 16, p. 32.

26 *Ibid.* I, 12–16; II, 2.

27 *Ibid.* I, 12 & 13, pp. 22–25.

BOOK III

The Layman on the Mind

Chapter I. *How a Philosopher visited the Layman so that he might learn more about the nature of the mind. How the mind is mind in itself, but through its function is a soul and is named from measuring.*

Of the many people going to Rome with wonderful devotion because of the jubilee,[1] it was reported that a Philosopher, who held the first place among all philosophers now alive, was to be found on a bridge admiring those crossing over. An Orator, most eager for knowledge, carefully searched for him. Upon recognizing him from the paleness of his face, his long toga and other things revealing the gravity of a thoughtful man, he greeted him gently and asked what caused him to remain in that place.

PHILOSOPHER: Wonder.

ORATOR: Wonder seems to be an incentive for all who strive to know anything whatever.[2] Therefore, I believe that it is a very great wonder that keeps you so engaged, since you are held to be the foremost amongst the learned.

PHILOSOPHER: Well said, friend. When I observe countless people from nearly every part of the world passing by in a great throng, I wonder at the one faith of all of them in such a diversity of bodies. Although no one of them is able to be like another, the faith of all of them is nonetheless one. It has brought them by such devotion from the ends of the earth.

ORATOR: Certainly a gift of God is necessary for laymen to attain more clearly by faith what philosophers attain by reason. You surely know how great the work of inquiry is, to study by reason the immortality of the mind. Yet by their faith alone none of these people holds this to be a matter for doubt. All of their concern and labour tends to this: that their souls after death, darkened by no sin, be taken into the luminous and most desirable life.

PHILOSOPHER: You say something both great and true, my friend. In wandering throughout the world I have spent all of my time searching out the wise so that I might be more certain about the immortality of the mind. At Delphi, knowledge was prescribed so that the mind may know itself and realize that it is joined with the divine mind.[3] But I have yet to attain my quest so perfectly and clearly with reason as these ignorant people have with faith.

ORATOR: If it is permitted, please explain what moved you, who seem to be a Peripatetic, to come to Rome. Can it be that you think that you will find here someone from whom you may learn?

PHILOSOPHER: I had heard that many writings of wise men are to be found here in the temple on the Capital dedicated by T. Attilius Crassus to Mens.[4] But perhaps I have come in vain, unless you, who seem to me to be both a good and knowledgeable citizen, offer to help.

ORATOR: Crassus did indeed dedicate a temple of Mens. No one would know, however, whether there were writings on the mind in that temple and which they were, after so many disasters in Rome. But so that you may not lament having come in vain, you will hear a layman, in my judgement most wonderful, about whatever you want.

PHILOSOPHER: I pray that this be done as soon as possible.

ORATOR: Follow me then.

When they were near the Temple of Eternity they descended into a little underground room and there the Orator addressed the Layman who was carving a spoon out of wood.

ORATOR: Layman, I blush because this great philosopher finds you involved in such rustic tasks. He will not believe that he will hear any theories from you.

LAYMAN: I am glad to be occupied in these tasks that constantly nourish both the mind and the body. I think that if this man whom you have brought is a philosopher, he will not scorn me because I am occupied in the art of spoon-carving.

PHILOSOPHER: Well spoken. Even Plato is reported to have painted once in a while. It is believed that he never would have done so if it had been adverse to speculation.

ORATOR: Maybe that is why examples from the art of painting were familiar to Plato who used them to make great things easy.

LAYMAN: Indeed, in my art I seek symbolically what I want, and feed my mind. I sell the spoons to replenish the body. And so I attain as much as is sufficient of all the things that I need.

PHILOSOPHER: It is my custom when I approach a man famous for wisdom to be solicitous first of all about the things that trouble me, to produce writings and to inquire about their meaning. However, because you are a layman, I do not know how to induce you to speak so that I may discover what you understand about the mind.

LAYMAN: I believe that there is no one more easily urged to speak about what he thinks than I am. Since I confess that I am an ignorant layman, I am not afraid to answer anything. Learned philosophers and those famous for knowledge rightly deliberate more carefully because they fear falling into error.[5] Therefore, if you tell me plainly what you want from me, you will receive it simply.

PHILOSOPHER: I cannot explain this briefly. If it is acceptable to you, let us sit down and speak casually.

LAYMAN: That will be good.

Footstools were placed in a triangle and the three men took their places. Then the Orator spoke.

ORATOR: You see, Philosopher, the simplicity of this man. He has none of the things that decency requires for the reception of such an important man. Test him on those questions that most trouble you. He will conceal nothing from you that he knows about them, and you will find, I believe, that you have not been brought here in vain.

PHILOSOPHER: So far I am satisfied with everything. Let us now come to the point. I beg you to be silent in the meantime, and do not allow the lengthy conversation to tire you.

ORATOR: You will find that I am eager for its continuation rather than bored by it.

PHILOSOPHER: Tell me then, Layman, for so you call yourself, whether you have a conjecture[6] about the mind.

LAYMAN: I think that there is not nor ever was a mature[7] human being who did not form at least some concept of the mind. Indeed, I also have one: the mind is that from which comes the limit and the measure of all things. In fact, I conjecture that the term "mind" (*mens*) is derived from the term for measuring (*mensurando*).[8]

PHILOSOPHER: Do you think that the mind is one thing and the soul another?

LAYMAN: I certainly do think so. There is one mind subsisting in itself; there is another which is in the body. The mind as it subsists in itself is either infinite or the image of the infinite. I admit that some of these minds that are the image of the infinite are able to animate human bodies because they are not maximum and absolute nor infinite and subsisting in themselves. I then grant that they are souls by virtue of this function.

PHILOSOPHER: You grant, therefore, that the mind and the soul of man are the same; the mind in itself, the soul by virtue of its function?

LAYMAN: I admit it, just as the sensitive power and the visual power
of the eye are one in an animal.

Chapter II. *How there is a natural word and another word imposed ac-*
cording to the natural word but without precision. How there is a simple
principle that is the art of arts. How the eternal art of philosophers is
enfolded.[9]

PHILOSOPHER: You said that the mind is named from measuring. I
have never read of anyone who has held this point among the
various derivations of the word. So first of all I ask you to reveal
the reason for this claim.

LAYMAN: If it is necessary to investigate more diligently the force of
the word, then I think that that power, which is in us and which
conceptually enfolds the exemplars of all things,[10] and which I
call "mind," is by no means properly named. For just as human
reason does not attain the essence of the word of God, neither
does a word. Words are imposed by the action of reason; we
name something by one word for a given reason, and the same
thing by a different word for a different reason. One language has
words that are appropriate while another language has those that
are crude and more inappropriate. And because the propriety of
words admits of a more and a less, I see that precise designation
is unknown.

PHILOSOPHER: You hasten into deep things, Layman. According to
what you seem to say, words are less appropriate because they
are, as you suppose, instituted at pleasure, just as it occurred to
someone by the action of his reason.[11]

LAYMAN: I want you to understand me more deeply! I admit that
every word is so united, as the form comes to the matter and truly
brings the word into being, that words are not by imposition, but
from eternity. Although an imposition is free, nevertheless I do
not think that there is any other than an appropriate name imposed,
although it may not be precise.

PHILOSOPHER: Please make yourself clearer so that I may grasp your
meaning.

LAYMAN: With pleasure. I turn now to this art of spoon-making. I
want you to know at the very outset that I claim without hesitation
that all human arts are but images of the infinite and divine art. I

do not know whether you agree.

PHILOSOPHER: You demand profound things and it is not proper to respond to them casually.

LAYMAN: I wonder if you have ever read a philosopher who did not know this, because it is evident. It is obvious that no human art has attained the precision of perfection and every one of them is finite and limited. One art is limited within its limits and another within its other limits. Each art is different from the others and no one art enfolds all the arts.[12]

PHILOSOPHER: What inference follows from this?

LAYMAN: The inference that every human art is finite.

PHILOSOPHER: Who doubts this?

LAYMAN: It is impossible, moreover, that there be a plurality of infinites that are in reality distinct.[13]

PHILOSOPHER: I admit this because one of them would be limited by another.

LAYMAN: If this is so, it must follow that the absolute principle alone is infinite because there is no principle prior to this principle, as is obvious. Otherwise the principle would be derived. Thus eternity is itself the only infinity or the absolute principle.

PHILOSOPHER: I admit that.

LAYMAN: Therefore, only unique absolute eternity is infinity. It is without principle and thus everything finite receives its principle from the infinite principle.

PHILOSOPHER: I cannot deny it.

LAYMAN: Thus every finite art is from the infinite art. And so the infinite art must be the exemplar of all arts, their principle, medium, end, standard,[14] measure, truth, precision, and perfection.

PHILOSOPHER: Continue to the point toward which you hasten, because no one is able to object to these things.

LAYMAN: I shall then apply symbolic examples from this art of spoon-making in order that what I say may be more apparent.[15]

PHILOSOPHER: I beg you to do this. I perceive that you hold the way to those things for which I yearn.

Having taken a spoon in his hand the Layman spoke

LAYMAN: The spoon has no other exemplar outside the idea in our mind. Although a sculptor or a painter may derive his exemplars from the things that he endeavors to represent, I do not do this when I make spoons and bowls from wood and pots from clay.

For in this I do not copy the figure of any natural thing. Only through human art are forms such as spoons, bowls, and pots perfected. Therefore, my art is more the perfecting than the copying of created figures[16] and in this is more like infinite art.

PHILOSOPHER: That pleases me.

LAYMAN: What I wish to do, therefore, is to explicate the art and to render sensible the form of spoonness,[17] through which a spoon is constituted. Because this form is neither black nor white nor any other colour nor a sound nor a smell nor taste nor touch, it is not attainable in its own nature by any sense. Nevertheless, I shall attempt to make it sensible in the mode in which it can be done.[18] And so by the different movements of my tools that I apply to the matter, for example a piece of wood, I shape and carve until there appears the due proportion in which the form of spoonness consistently shines forth.[19] Thus you see the simple and non-sensible form of spoonness shine forth in the formed proportion of this wood as in its image. The truth and precision of spoonness can therefore be neither multiplied nor communicated and is not able to be made fully sensible by means of any tools or man.

In all spoons nothing except the most simple form shines forth in different ways, greater in one and less in another, but in none with precision. The wood receives its name from the form attained,[20] so that when the proportion appears in which spoonness shines forth, it is called a "spoon," and the name is united to the form. Nonetheless, the imposition of the name is arbitrary because another name could have been imposed. Even though the imposed name is arbitrary, it is not completely different from the natural name united to the form. After the form is attained the natural designation shines forth in all of the different names variously imposed by any of the nations. The imposition of the designation is therefore accomplished by the action of reason.[21]

The action of reason is related to the things that are known by the senses. Of these, the reason makes discretion, likeness, and difference, with the result that nothing is in the reason that was not first in the senses. Therefore, reason names things and is moved to give this name for one thing, another for something else. Because the form in its truth is not found in these things with which reason occupies itself, reason descends to conjecture and opinion. Accordingly, genera and species, as designated by names, are beings of the reason made by reason for itself from the likeness and difference of sensible things. Being posterior by nature to the sensible things of which they are likenesses, they cannot continue to exist should the sensible things be destroyed.

Thus, whoever holds that nothing can belong to the intellect that is not also in the reason, also holds that nothing can belong to the intellect that was not first in the senses. He must necessarily say that a thing is nothing unless it is named, and in every analysis his effort is to probe the names. Such analysis is enjoyable to a man because it proceeds by the action of the reason. This man would then deny that forms in themselves and in their truth exist separately otherwise than insofar as they are beings of the reason. Exemplars and Ideas are held to be nothing.

But those who admit that there is something in the mind's understanding[22] that was neither in the senses nor in the reason, namely the exemplary and incommunicable truth of the forms that shine forth in sensible things, claim that exemplars precede sensible things by nature, as truth precedes its image. They define the order as follows: first in the order of nature is humanity, existing in and of itself, namely without prior matter. Then there is man existing through humanity and included in its designation. Finally, there is the species that exists in the reason. Were all men to be destroyed, humanity, as a species that is included in the designation and as a being of the reason sought after by reason from the likeness of man, could not subsist. It would depend upon men who did not exist.

The humanity, however, through which men did exist does not cease because of this dependence. Humanity does not belong to the designation of the species, insofar as the designations are imposed by the action of the reason. Instead, it is the truth of that species belonging to the designation. If the image is destroyed the truth in itself remains. All these men deny that a thing is nothing other than what belongs to the designation, even though logic and rational consideration about things proceeds according to the mode of designation.

Therefore, they inquire by means of logic, explaining and praising, but not resting there, because reason or logic is concerned only with the images of forms. They try to see things theologically, beyond the force of designation, and turn to the exemplars and ideas. I do not think any more modes of inquiry can be given. If you who are a philosopher have read other opinions you would know of them. I conjecture that there are no others.

PHILOSOPHER: You have admirably touched upon all the sects of the philosophers, Peripatetics as well as Academics.

LAYMAN: Once the mind raises itself to infinity all these differences, as many as can be thought of, are easily resolved and harmonized. As the Orator who is present will explain to you in more detail, from the things he has heard from me, the infinite form alone is one and most simple. It shines forth in all things as the most adequate exemplar of each and every formable thing. Thus it will certainly be true that there are not many separate exemplars and Ideas of things. Indeed, no reason is able to attain an infinite form. Being ineffable, it is not comprehended by any of the designations imposed by the operation of reason. Consequently, when a thing belongs to a designation, it is an image of its ineffable, proper, and adequate exemplar.

There is then one ineffable word that is the precise name of all things when they are included in a designation by the operation of reason. This ineffable name shines forth in all names in its own mode because it is the infinite appellation of all names and the infinite articulation of all the things that can be articulated by the voice. Thus every name is an image of the precise name. All the sects of philosophers have endeavoured to say nothing other than this, although what they have said could have been expressed better and more clearly. They have all agreed out of necessity that there is one infinite power, whom we call God, in whom all things are necessarily enfolded. And he who said that humanity, when it is not included in a designation, is the precision of truth, meant to say nothing other than that it is the ineffable infinite form. We call this infinite form, when we are regarding the human form, the latter's precise exemplar. And thus the ineffable form, when we regard its images, is named by the names of all things according to the specific differences formed by our reason from the exemplifications. The one completely simple exemplar appears then to be a multitude of exemplars.

Chapter III. *How the philosophers are understood and brought into agreement. Concerning the name of God and its precision. How when one precise name is known all things are known. Concerning the sufficiency of things that can be known. How God's conceiving and ours* *differ.*

PHILOSOPHER: You have wonderfully elucidated the dictum of Tris-
megistus who said that God is named with the names of all things
and all things are named with the name of God.[23]

LAYMAN: Enfold being-named and naming in the coincidence of the
highest intellect and everything will become clear. This is because God is the precision of all things whatsoever. Thus if one
possessed precise knowledge of one thing, he would possess by
necessity the knowledge of all things. And so if the precise name
of one thing were known, the names of all things would be known
because precision is not outside of God. Hence, whoever attained
to one precision would attain to God, who is the truth of all things
that can be known.

ORATOR: Explain, please, about the precision of a name.

LAYMAN: You know, Orator, how we bring forth mathematical figures
from the power of the mind. So, when I wish to make triangularity
visible, I set down a figure in which I establish three angles in
order that in the figure so formed and proportioned triangularity
may shine forth. To this figure is united the designation that is
supposed to be a trigon. I claim, therefore, that if "trigon" is
the precise designation of the triangular figure, then I know the
precise designations of all polygons. For I would then know that
the designation of a four-angled figure must be "tetragon," of a
five-angled figure "pentagon," and so forth. From the knowledge
of one name, I recognize the figure named and all the polygons
that can be named, their differences and likenesses and all that can
be known about the subject. Likewise, I maintain that if I knew
the precise name of one of God's works, I would not be ignorant
of any name of any of God's works and of whatever could be
known. Because the Word of God is the precision of every name
that can be named, it is clear that each and every object can be
known only in the Word.

ORATOR: In your own way you have thoroughly explained this point.

PHILOSOPHER: Layman, you have developed a wonderful doctrine for
accommodating all the philosophers. While I listen to you I can
agree with you that none of the philosophers wished to say anything other than what you have said. None of them was able
to deny that God is infinite. In this dictum alone all the things
you have said are enfolded. This sufficiency of everything that is

knowable and communicable in any manner is wonderful. Proceed, however, more fully to the consideration of the mind and
explain why it is said that mind is from measure. Granted that
mind is derived from measure, what do you claim mind to be?

LAYMAN: You know how divine simplicity is the enfolding of all
things. The mind is the image of this enfolding simplicity.[24] So
if you call this divine simplicity the infinite mind, then it will be
the exemplar of our mind. If you say that the divine mind is the
universe of the truth of things, you will be stating that our mind is
the entirety of the assimilation of things in order to be the universe
of ideas.

The divine mind's conception is the bringing forth of things,[25]
whereas our mind's conception is the idea of things. If the divine
mind is absolute being, its conception is the creation of beings.
Conception for our mind is the assimilation of beings.[26] Those
things which are appropriate to the divine mind as infinite truth
are appropriate to our mind as its approximate image. If all things
are in the divine mind as in their precise and proper truth, then all
things are in our minds as in an image or similitude of the proper
truth, that is, conceptually. This is because cognition occurs by
means of similitude. All things are in God, but they exist in Him
as the exemplars of things. In our mind they exist as the similitude
of things. As God is absolute being, the enfolding of all beings,
so is our mind the image of that infinite being, enfolding all of
the images.

Our mind, like the first image of an unknown king, is the
exemplar for all other paintings of him. The acquaintance or the
visage of God does not descend except into a mental nature whose
object is truth. It proceeds no farther than to the mind. So it is
that the mind is the image of God and the exemplar of all of
the images of God subordinate to it. It follows that everything
subordinate to the simple mind participates in the mind insofar as
it concerns the image of God. Thus the mind is the image of God
through itself and everything subordinate to the mind is an image
only through the mind.

Chapter IV. *How our mind is an image and not an unfolding of eternal
enfolding. Those things that are subordinate to the mind are not an
image. How the mind is without ideas yet still has connate judgement.*

Why the body is necessary for the mind.

PHILOSOPHER: From the great plenitude of your mind you seem to
wish to say that the infinite mind is the absolute formative power
and the finite mind a conformative or configurative power.

LAYMAN: Yes, I wish it to be said in that manner. What is necessary to
say, however, cannot be appropriately expressed. A multiplication
of discourse is thus completely suitable. Notice that an image
is something different from an unfolding. Equality is an image
of unity, because equality arises out of unity taken once. Thus
equality is an image of unity, but it is not the unfolding of unity. It
is the plurality of the enfolded. Therefore, an image is an equality
of unity, not an unfolding. Similarly I wish to say that among all
the images of divine enfolding, the mind is the simplest image of
the divine mind. Consequently the mind is the first image of the
divine enfolding, uniting all the images of enfolding by means of
its simplicity and power.[27]

For just as God is the enfolding of the enfoldings, so is the
mind, which is the image of God, the image of the enfolding of the
enfoldings. Subordinate to the images are the pluralities of things
unfolding the divine enfolding, just as number is the unfolding of
unity, motion of rest, time of eternity, composition of simplicity,
time of the present, magnitude of the point, inequality of equality,
diversity of identity, and so forth.

From this image you should realize the wonderful power of
our mind. For enfolded in its power is the assimilative power
of the enfolding of the point, through which it finds in itself the
potency by which it assimilates itself to every magnitude. Because
of this power to assimilate whatever is enfolded in unity, the mind
is able to assimilate itself to every multitude. Thus it is able
to assimilate itself to all time through the assimilative power of
enfolding the now or the present. Likewise it can assimilate itself
to all motion through the assimilative power of enfolding rest, to
all composition from simplicity, to all diversity from identity, to
all inequality from equality, to all disjunction from connection.
Through the image of absolute enfolding, which is the infinite
mind, the mind has the power by which it is able to assimilate
itself to every unfolding. You see yourself that many similar
things can be said about what our mind has, because of its being
the image of the infinite simplicity which enfolds all things.

PHILOSOPHER: It appears that only the mind is the image of God.

LAYMAN: Properly it is, because all things that are subordinate to the mind are an image of God only insofar as the mind itself shines forth in them. For just as the mind shines forth more in the perfect animals than in those less perfect, it shines forth more in the sensitive than in the vegetative beings, and more in the vegetative beings than in minerals. Thus creatures without mind are the unfoldings rather than the images of the divine simplicity, even though they participate in various ways in the unfolding of the image according to the reflection of the mental image.

PHILOSOPHER: Aristotle said that there is no connate idea in our mind or soul[28] because he compared it to a blank tablet.[29] Plato said that there are connate ideas but, due to the mass of the body, the soul has forgotten them.[30] What do you think is the truth in this?

LAYMAN: Our mind has no doubt been put into this body by God for its progress. It is necessary, therefore, that it have from God everything needed to achieve progress. Consequently one should not believe that there are connate ideas in the soul that it lost in the body, but that the soul requires a body so that its connate power may proceed to act. The visual power of the soul cannot accomplish its operation, so that it may actually see, unless it is stimulated by an object. It cannot be stimulated except through the presentation of the species multiplied through the medium of the organ. Thus it needs the eye.

Similarly, the power of the mind, which is the power of comprehending things and ideas, cannot accomplish its operations unless it is stimulated by sensible things. It is not able to be stimulated except through mediations by sensible phantasms. Therefore, it needs an organic body of such a kind that stimulation could not take place without it. In this respect Aristotle appears to be correct in his opinion that connate ideas do not exist in the soul at its inception and that they are not lost when the soul entered the body. Like a deaf man who could never advance in playing the zither because he would possess no judgement of the harmony by which he would be able to judge his progress, the mind could not advance were it to be deprived of all judgement. Wherefore, our mind has within itself a connate judgement without which it could not advance. This judicial power is naturally connate to the mind, which uses it to judge in itself whether reasons are weak, strong, or conclusive. If this power is what Plato called a connate idea, he was not entirely in error.[31]

PHILOSOPHER: Your teaching is so plain that all who hear it are compelled to agree. Without a doubt it is necessary to attend closely to these things; clearly we experience the spirit speaking in our mind, judging that this is good, this is just and this is true, and castigating us if we are disinclined to the just. This language and judgement is in no way learned, but is connate to the mind.

LAYMAN: We prove from this that the mind is that power that, although it lacks every form of conception, still is able, once it is stimulated, to assimilate itself to every form and to produce ideas of all things. In a certain manner it is similar to the vision of a healthy man in darkness, who has never been in the light: he is without any actual idea of visible things. However, when he comes into the light and is stimulated, his vision assimilates itself to what is visible in order to make an idea.

ORATOR: Plato once said that a judgement is required from the intellect when the senses simultaneously produce contraries.[32]

LAYMAN: He spoke correctly. When the sense of touch confusedly offers simultaneously something hard and soft, or heavy and light, one contrary with another, the situation is referred to the intellect in order to judge the essence of both to see if the confused sensation may be better distinguished. So when sight confusedly presents something as large and small, is not the distinguishing judgement of the intellect necessary to decide what is large and what is small? When the sense is sufficient in itself, there would be no recourse to the judgement of the intellect, as in seeing a finger, which has no contrary appearing simultaneously.

Chapter V. How the mind is a living substance and is created in the body. Concerning the manner in which this happens. Whether there is reason in brute animals. How the mind is the living description of eternal wisdom.

PHILOSOPHER: Almost all Peripatetics say that the intellect, which you seem to call mind, is a certain potency of the soul and that understanding[33] is an accident. You, however, think otherwise.

LAYMAN: The mind is a living substance that we experience within ourselves as an internal speaking and judging.[34] It is assimilated more to the infinite substance and absolute form than are any of all the other spiritual powers that we experience within ourselves. Its purpose in a particular body is to vivify the body and therefore it is called the soul.[35] Thus the mind is a substantial form or power, enfolding all things in itself according to its own mode. It enfolds the power of animation, through which it animates the body with a vegetative and sensitive life, and is a rational, intellectual and intelligible power.

PHILOSOPHER: Do you want to say that the mind, which you claim is an intellective soul, exists before the body and is incorporated later? This is what Pythagoras and the Platonists maintain.[36]

LAYMAN: It exists before the body according to nature, but not in time. I have compared the mind to vision in darkness, as you have heard. Vision, however, is never in act before the eye exists, yet is prior to the eye in nature. Because the mind is a certain divine seed,[37] conceptually enfolding the exemplars of all things through its own power, God, from whom it has this power and its being, has simultaneously located it in suitable soil where it could bear fruit and conceptually unfold from itself the totality of things. If it did not have the occasion to appear in act, this seminal power would have been given to the mind in vain.

PHILOSOPHER: You speak with authority. I very much desire, however, to learn how this was produced in us.

LAYMAN: The divine modes are unattainable in their precision. Nevertheless, we make conjectures about them, some more obscure, others more clear. I think that the following analogy, which I shall relate, will be sufficient for you. You realize that vision by its own proper nature does not discriminate, but, in a certain area, senses in a confused way an object presented that it meets within its own sphere of motion, namely in the eye. The object presented is generated from the multiplication of the appearances of the object in the eye. So, if vision is in the eye without discretion, as in infants where the use of discretion is absent, then the mind comes to the sensible soul as discretion does to vision, when it uses it to discern colours. This visual discretion is found in the perfect brutes, as in dogs that discern their masters by sight. It is given to vision by God as its form and perfection. Thus a higher power has been given to human nature, beyond that found in the brutes, yet related to the discretion of animals as animal discretion is related to the power of sense. From this it follows that the mind is the form of animal discretion and is its perfection.

PHILOSOPHER: Well and good. But you appear to accept the opinion of the wise man Philo who said that there was reason in animals.

LAYMAN: We observe in brutes a discriminative operation. Without it, their natures could not subsist. Lacking form, namely intellect or mind, their operation is confused. The animal does not have judgement and knowledge. But insofar as all discretion proceeds from reason, Philo does not seem to have spoken nonsense.

PHILOSOPHER: Please make clear how the mind is the form of discursive reason.

LAYMAN: I have already explained that vision sees and does not realize what it sees until discretion informs, elucidates, and perfects it. Similarly, reason syllogizes and does not realize what it syllogizes about until the mind informs, elucidates, and perfects it. Then it knows what it is syllogizing about. If a layman ignorant of the power of words were to read some books, the reading would come from the power of reason. Although he would not know what he is reading, he would read by going over the differences among the letters, combining and separating them. But this is the work of reason. There may be another man who reads and knows, as well as understands, what he is reading. This is a kind of analogy of confused reason as opposed to reason that is informed by the mind. For the mind has a faculty of judgement that discerns reasons in order to determine which ones are good and which ones are sophistical. Thus, the mind is the discerning form of reasons in the same way that reason is the discerning form of the senses and of the imagination.

PHILOSOPHER: From what does the mind have this judgement, since it appears to make judgements about everything?

LAYMAN: The mind has judgement because it is the image of the exemplar of all things. Now God is the exemplar of all things. Thus, because the exemplar of all things shines forth in the mind as truth in its image, the mind has within itself the reference that it employs in judging external things. If the written law were a living thing, it would, by being alive, read in itself the judgements that must be given. Therefore, the mind is a living description of eternal and infinite wisdom. In our minds the beginning of this life is similar to a sleeping man when he is aroused and stimulated to wonder by sensible things: he is moved by the action of his own intellectual life,[38] and finds described within himself what he is seeking. You must realize, however, that this description is

a reflection[39] of the exemplar of all things in the way in which
truth is reflected in its image. If the simplest indivisible point of
an angle on a highly polished diamond, in which the forms of all
things were reflected, were alive, it would discover by looking into
itself the likenesses of all things. By means of these likenesses it
would be able to make ideas about everything.

PHILOSOPHER: You speak wonderfully and offer things that are very
pleasant to hear about. The example of the point of the diamond
pleases me very much. For the sharper and simpler the angle, the
more clearly all things are reflected in it.

LAYMAN: If anyone contemplates the mirror-like power within himself,
he will see how it is prior to all quantity. He who conceives it to
be alive with an intellectual life in which the exemplar of all things
shines forth, makes an acceptable conjecture about the mind.

PHILOSOPHER: I would like to learn whether you can apply your own
art as a paradigm of the creation of the mind.

LAYMAN: Yes, I can.

And taking a beautiful spoon in his hand, he said:

LAYMAN: I wished to make a mirror-like spoon. I looked for wood
that was hard and finer than all others. I applied my instruments
and by their use I brought forth an appropriate proportion in which
the form of a spoon was perfectly reflected. I then polished the
surface of the spoon until, as you see, I introduced a mirror-like
form into the reflection of the form of the spoon. Even though it
is a very beautiful spoon, it is also a spoon that is like a mirror.
For you have in it every kind of mirror: concave, convex, flat,
and cylindrical. It is flat at the base of the handle, cylindrical in
the handle, concave in the hollow of the spoon and convex in the
back. Thus, the mirror-like form did not have a temporal existence
before the spoon. That was added by me to the first form of the
spoon to perfect it, so that now the mirror-like form might contain
in itself the form of the spoon. The mirror-like form does not
depend on the spoon, because it is not of the essence of a mirror
to be a spoon. Wherefore, the spoon would cease to exist if the
proportions were destroyed without which the form of the spoon
could not exist. But the mirror-like form would not cease to exist
if, for example, the handle of the spoon were broken. Similarly,
from the appropriate matter God drew forth through the motion of
the heavens the proportion in which animality might be reflected

in a more perfect mode. Then He added mind to it as a living mirror in the manner I have already explained.

Chapter VI. How wise men, speaking figuratively, have said that number is the exemplar of all things. Concerning the wonderful nature of number. How number is derived from the mind and from the incorruptibility of essences. How the mind is a harmony, a self-moving number,[40] a composition of identity and diversity.

PHILOSOPHER: You have aptly applied your art as a paradigm. When you state that there is one intellect, you demonstrate the production of things and explain how proportion is the realm, sphere or region of forms, while matter is the realm of proportion. You certainly appear to be like those Pythagoreans who assert that all things are derived from number.

LAYMAN: I do not know whether I am a Pythagorean or something else. But I know this: no authority leads me, even if it tries to move me. However, I think that the Pythagoreans, who, as you claim, philosophize about all things through number, are great and astute men. I do not believe that they wished to speak about number as an abstraction[41] that proceeds from our mind. For it is evident that this is not the principle of anything. Instead, they spoke figuratively and rationally about number as it proceeds from the divine mind, of which abstract number is an image. As our mind is related to the infinite and eternal mind, the number of our mind is related to the number of the divine mind. We give the name of our mind to that mind in the same way that we give our name to the divine number. With great delight we occupy ourselves in number as with a task that is appropriate to us.

PHILOSOPHER: Explain please the reasons that can move someone to say that numbers are the principles of things.

LAYMAN: Only one infinite principle can exist. It alone is infinitely simple. The first inchoate being[42] cannot be infinitely simple, as is self-evident. Nor can it be composed of other parts, because it would then not be the first inchoate being; its parts would precede it in nature. Therefore, it is necessary to admit that the first inchoate being is composed of itself and not out of other things. Our mind does not comprehend how such a thing is able to exist, unless it be a number or exist as the number of our mind.

Number, in fact, is composed out of itself, since every number is a composite of an even and an odd number. Thus number is composed out of number. If you said that the number three is composed out of three units, you would be speaking the way someone does who claims that walls and a roof make a house when they still exist separately. For if the walls and the roof are separate, no house is composed from them. Therefore, three units do not separately constitute the number three. So if you consider unities as they constitute the number three, you are considering them to be a unity. What then are three united unities, but the number three? Accordingly, it is composed of itself. The same is true for all numbers.

While I perceive nothing in number but unity, I see the incomposite composition of number as well as the coincidence of simplicity and composition or of unity and multiplicity. Indeed, if I observe more accurately, I see the composite unity of number as in the harmonic unity of an octave, a fifth and a fourth. A harmonic relation is a unity that cannot be understood without number. I also see from the relation of a semitone and a double-half, which is that of the side of a square to its diameter, that there is a number more simple than our mind's reason can attain. For without number a relation is not understood. Nevertheless, that number must also be either even or odd. If we were not hastening on to other things, it would be possible to have a long and pleasant conversation about this number.

We have thus learned how the first inchoate being exists, and that it is a type of number. Because the precision of the essence of anything is not attainable by us except in an enigma or figure, we are not able to draw nearer to the essence of this being. We name the first inchoate being figuratively when we call it number because number is the subject of proportion.

Without number, it is not possible for proportion to exist. Proportion is the realm of form, for without a proportion suitable and adapted to a form, the form is not able to appear. As I have said, the form of the spoon is not able to remain once the proportion suitable to it is ruined. It would not have a location. Its proportion is like the aptitude of the surface of the mirror for the reflection of an image. Once this fails, the representation ceases to exist. Observe the way in which the infinite unity of an exemplar is able to appear only in a suitable proportion. Number is such a proportion. The eternal mind functions the way a musician does when he wishes to make manifest his intention. He takes a multitude of voices and brings them into the concordant proportion of a harmony. In this proportion the harmony appears sweetly and perfectly when it is there as in its own realm. The reflection of the harmony is varied according to the variety of the concordant proportion of the harmony. This harmony ceases to exist once the aptitude of the proportion comes to an end. Thus, number and all things are derived from the mind.

PHILOSOPHER: Would there not be a plurality of things without the consideration of our mind?

LAYMAN: Yes, but the plurality would be due to the eternal mind. Thus, as the plurality of things exists with respect to God because of the divine mind, it exists for us because of our mind. For the mind alone enumerates things, and, if it is removed, number ceases to be a distinct thing. The mind is truly the equality of unity since it understands one and the same thing both separately and singly[43] under a sign. When we consider something, we say that it is one thing when the mind understands it separately.[44] Because the mind understands one thing separately and multiplies it, we determine that there are many things. We say that there are two things when the mind understands separately one and the same thing twice or doubly. And so on for the rest.

PHILOSOPHER: Is not a ternary number composed from a binary number and unity?[45] Do we call a number a collection of singulars? Why then do you claim that number is derived from the mind?

LAYMAN: Such modes of speaking should be referred to the mode of understanding. Arithmetic addition is nothing but the multiplication of the same things with reference to something common. So once you see that without the mind, a binary or a ternary number is nothing, you realize that number is derived from the mind.

PHILOSOPHER: In what way is the plurality of things the number of the divine mind?

LAYMAN: The plurality of things comes into being because the divine mind understands one thing in one way and another thing in another way. If you consider carefully, you will find that the plurality of things is nothing but a mode of the divine mind's understanding. Thus I conjecture that it can be maintained without objection that number is the first exemplar of things in the spirit of the creator.[46] This shows that delight and beauty, which are in all

things, are the result of the proportion that is number. It follows
then that the particular path leading to wisdom is number.[47]

PHILOSOPHER: The Pythagoreans said this first, followed by the Platonists, whom Boethius imitated.

LAYMAN: Likewise, I assert that number is the exemplar of our mind's
concepts. Without number, the mind cannot do anything. Neither
assimilation, conception, discretion, nor measurement would occur
if number did not exist. In the absence of number, things cannot be
understood as separate and discrete.[48] Nor, without number, is one
thing understood to be a substance, another a quality, and so on for
the other categories.[49] Consequently, nothing can be understood
without number because it is the mode of understanding. Our
mind's number is the exemplar of its ideas, because it is an image
of the divine number that is the exemplar of things. As unity is
prior to all plurality, its act of unification[50] is the uncreated mind
in which all things are one. Plurality comes after the one as the
unfolding of that unity's power. This power is the entity of things,
the equality of being, and the connection of entity and equality,
which is the Blessed Trinity. As a result, the image of the divine
Trinity is in our mind. Our mind is like a uniting unity preceding
all plurality conceivable by the mind. Following the unity that
unites all plurality is the plurality that is the image of the plurality
of things. In the same way, our mind is the image of the divine
mind. Furthermore, plurality unfolds the mind's power of unity,
which is the image of entity, equality and connection.

PHILOSOPHER: I perceive that you attain wonderful things from numbers. The divine Dionysius claims that the essence of things are
incorruptible.[51] Are you able to prove this through number?

LAYMAN: When you consider that number consists of a unity derived
from a multitude and that difference[52] is contingent upon multiplication, you notice that the composition of number is derived from
unity and difference, from identity and diversity, from the even
and the odd, from the divided and the undivided. The essence of
all things originated as a number of the divine mind. In a way,
you attain to the manner in which the essences of things are incorruptible, as is unity, from which comes number. This unity is
an entity. You grasp the way in which things exist in one manner
or another, because of difference. Difference, however, is not due
to the essence of number, but depends upon the multiplication
of unity. Difference certainly does not belong to the essence of

anything; it pertains rather to annihilation, since it is the division that gives rise to corruption. Consequently, it is not the essence of anything. In addition, you notice how number is nothing other than the things that are enumerated. From this fact you know that number, insofar as it really exists, does not intervene between the divine mind and things. Rather, the number of things are the things.

Chapter VII. *How the mind, by means of assimilation, reveals from itself the forms of things. How it attains absolute possibility of matter.*

PHILOSOPHER: Please tell me. Do you think that our mind is a harmony, or a self-moving number? Is it a composition of the same and the diverse, or of a divided and undivided essence? Or is it an entelechy? Both the Platonists and the Peripatetics use such modes of speaking.[53]

LAYMAN: I think that all those men who have spoken about the mind could have said these or other things. They were motivated by what they encountered in the power of the mind. They learned that the mind possesses a judgement with respect to every harmony and formulates ideas out of itself. The mind, therefore, moves itself as though it were a living discerning number, producing distinctions by itself. It proceeds to do this either collectively and distributively, or according to the mode of simplicity and absolute necessity, or by absolute possibility, or through the necessity of comprehension or determination, or through determinate possibility, or from an aptitude for perpetual activity. Because of these and various experiences that are similar, it is reasonable to believe remarks such as these, as well as other things said about the mind or the soul. To say that the mind exists in relation to the same and the diverse is to assert that it exists in relation to unity and difference. This mode of existence is identical with that of number, which is said to be composed of the same with respect to the universal and of the diverse with respect to particulars. These are the modes of the mind's understanding.

PHILOSOPHER: Proceed now to the explanation of the soul as a self-moving number.

LAYMAN: I will do what I can. I believe that no one would be able to deny that the mind is a kind of living, divine number that is well

suited for the reflection of divine harmony. No one could deny that
the mind enfolds every sensible, rational, and intellectual harmony,
and whatever can be said in the order of beauty. However, every
number, proportion, and harmony that proceeds from our mind
approaches no nearer to our mind than our mind does to the infinite
mind. Although the mind is a divine number, it is nevertheless
a number that is a simple unity that reveals its number out of its
own power. Consequently, the proportion that exists between God
and His works is identical to the proportion that exists between
our mind and its works.

PHILOSOPHER: Many men have thought that our mind is of a divine
nature, nearly united to the divine mind.[54]

LAYMAN: I do not believe that they intended to say anything different
from what I have said, although they have used a different way of
speaking. The difference between the divine mind and our mind
is the distinction between making and seeking. The divine mind
creates by means of conception, while our mind assimilates ideas
or produces intellectual images. The divine mind is the power of
generating being;[55] our mind has the power of assimilating being.

ORATOR: I realize that the Philosopher does not have enough time, so
for some time I have held myself back in silence. I have heard
many things that are pleasing; now I would like to hear how the
mind reveals the forms of things by assimilation.

LAYMAN: The mind is so assimilative that it assimilates to itself visible things in vision, audible things in hearing, tastable things in
tasting, odour in smelling, tangible things in touching; in sensation
it assimilates to itself sensible things, in imagination it assimilates
the things that can be imagined, while in reason it assimilates the
objects of reason. In the absence of sensible things, the faculty of
imagination[56] is similar to a sense faculty that lacks the discretion
of sensible objects. It conforms itself to sensible objects that are
absent in a confused manner, without discerning one state from
another. In the reason, however, the faculty of imagination conforms itself to things by discerning one condition from another. In
all of these situations our mind is carried in the spirit of the arteries where it is stimulated by the obstacle of species. The species
are multiplied from the objects to the spirit, which assimilates itself to things by means of species, so as to make a judgement
of the object through the assimilation. This subtle spirit of the
arteries is animated[57] therefore by the mind which conforms it to

the similitude of the species.

The species, however, present an obstacle to the action of the spirit. The spirit is conformed to the obstacle, just as pliable wax is formed by a man having both mind and art into an object actually present to the artist. For everything that is put into a configuration, whether by the art of sculpture, painting or hammering, could not be made without the mind. It is the mind that limits all things. Therefore, if a piece of wax were conceived as being informed by the mind, the indwelling mind would make it conform to every figure presented to it, just as the mind of an artist attempts to do through external application. The same thing could be said about clay and all pliable matter. In our body, therefore, the mind produces various configurations, both subtle and coarse, in concurrence with the diverse pliability of the arterial spirits in the organs. One spirit is not configurable to that to which another spirit is configurable, because the spirit in the optic nerve is not encountered through the species of sounds, but only through the species of colours. Thus, it is configurable to the species of colours and not to sounds. The same is true for the other species. In the organ of imagination there is another spirit that is configurable to all sensible species, although in a mode that is unrefined and indistinct. There is also a spirit in the rational organ; it is configurable to everything sensible in a distinct and clear manner. All of these configurations are assimilations of sensible objects, because they are produced through the medium of very subtle corporeal spirits.

Although the mind generates these assimilations so as to possess ideas of sensible objects and is thus immersed in a corporeal spirit, it functions as a soul animating a body. By means of this animation, an animal is produced. The soul of brute animals produces assimilations according to its own mode. These assimilations are similar to, but more confused than ours, attaining ideas in their own way.

The power of our mind, through assimilation derived from such ideas, produces the mechanical arts as well as physical and logical conjectures. The mind attains things according to the mode in which they are conceived as being in possibility or matter, and according to the mode in which they are possible beings, determined through form.[58] Because the mind attains only the ideas of sensible beings through these assimilations, in which the forms of things are not true but obscured by the variability of matter, all such ideas are more conjectures than truths. For this reason I maintain that ideas that are attained through rational assimilations are uncertain. They are identified more with the images of forms than with truths.

Moreover, our mind, not as immersed in the body that it animates, but as it exists in itself, though still capable of being united to a body, may reflect upon its own immutability. When it does this, it produces assimilations of forms, insofar as they are not immersed in matter but exist in and by themselves. It conceives the immutable essences of things by employing itself as an instrument, without any organic spirit. The mind conceives a circle as a figure from whose centre all lines leading to the circumference are equal. According to this mode of being, a circle cannot exist outside of the mind in matter; it is not possible for two material lines to be equal. It is even less possible that such a circle exists. Consequently, the circle as it is formed in the mind is the exemplar and measure of the truth of the circle on the pavement.[59] We maintain then that the truth of things in the mind is in the necessity of comprehension,[60] namely in the mode required by the truth of things, as was said about the circle.

The mind, in producing these assimilations in itself in abstraction from matter, assimilates itself to the abstracted forms. It reveals through this power the mathematically certain sciences and learns that it has the power to assimilate and generate ideas with respect to things that exist in the necessity of comprehension. The mind is stimulated through phantasms or the images of forms to approach these abstract assimilations. It apprehends these phantasms through the assimilations produced in the organs. It is similar to someone so stimulated by the beauty of an image that he seeks out the beauty of its exemplar. In this assimilation, it is as if the mind has a pliability that is independent of wax, clay, metal, and everything pliable. The mind is alive with a mental life, so that it is able to assimilate itself to all figures as they exist in themselves and not as they subsist in matter. In the power of its living pliability, existing in itself, the mind would realize that the ideas of all things exist because it is able to conform itself to all of them.

However, the mind is not satisfied by this mode because it does not intuit the precise truth of all things. What it does intuit is truth according to a particular necessity determined for each thing with respect to one thing existing according to one mode, another thing in a different mode, and each composed of its own parts. The mind realizes that truth itself is not identified with this mode of being, which is only a participation in truth in which one thing truly exists in one mode and another in a different mode. Such differences in modes can never be appropriate to truth in itself when it is considered in its infinite and absolute precision.

Consequently, the mind in considering its own simplicity, not only as abstracted from matter but as neither communicable to matter nor able to be united in the manner of form, uses this simplicity as an instrument in order to assimilate itself to all things. It does this not in abstraction from matter, but in a simplicity that cannot be communicated to matter. In this way the mind intuits all things in its own simplicity, just as it sees all magnitude in the point, and the circle in its centre. It intuits in its own simplicity all things without any composition of parts. The mind intuits things not as one thing exists in one mode and another in a different mode, but as all things are one and one thing is all. This is the intuition of absolute truth.

Just as if anyone saw, in the mode that we have just described, the manner in which all beings participate in various ways in entity, and he then intuited absolute entity itself beyond all participation and variety, in the mode that we are now describing, he would see all the things that had been seen in variety. Now, however, he would see them beyond the determined necessity of comprehension, in absolute and most simple necessity, without number, magnitude, and any difference. The mind itself uses this highest mode of intuition because it is the image of God.

God, who is all things, is reflected in the mind, when, as a living image of God, it turns to its exemplar, assimilating itself to it by every effort. In this way the minds sees immediately[61] that all things are one. It also sees that it is itself an assimilation of this one and that it forms ideas about the one that is all things by means of this assimilation. It thus produces theological speculations in which it reposes with great joy. For here it finds the limit of every idea, as in the most delightful truth of its own life. One cannot say too much about this mode of discourse. I have, however, related these things in a brief and simple manner. You will be able to make them more beautiful by a proper polishing, so that they will be more pleasing to readers.

ORATOR: I have eagerly waited to hear the very things that you have explained with such great clarity. Your words will seem sufficiently ornate for those who are seeking the truth.

PHILOSOPHER: Explain please how the mind attains the indeterminate possibility called matter.

LAYMAN: It does this through a sort of false reasoning. For it is contrary to the mode by which the mind rapidly proceeds from the necessity of comprehension to absolute necessity. The mind sees how all bodies have an existence formed through corporeity; were corporeity to be removed, the mind would see everything that it had seen before in a sort of indeterminate possibility. What it had seen before in a distinct and determinate corporeity in actual existence, it sees now as a confused, indeterminate possibility. This is a mode of universality, according to which everything appears to be possible. But because the ability to exist[62] does not itself exist, this is not a mode of being.

Chapter VIII. *How conceiving, understanding, and producing ideas and assimilations are the same thing for the mind. How sensations are produced according to philosophers of nature.*

PHILOSOPHER: Enough of this. Let us not go beyond what we proposed to discuss. Explain whether the mind's conceiving is identical with its understanding.

LAYMAN: I have said that the mind is the power of conceiving. When it is stimulated, it moves itself by an act of conception until it understands. Therefore, the perfect motion of the mind is that of the intellect.

PHILOSOPHER: When is the mind said to conceive?

LAYMAN: When it produces similitudes of things, which you may prefer to call either ideas or genera, differences, species, properties, and accidents. Thus God created the power of conception in the soul, but the mind produces the things we just mentioned. The power of the mind, however, is identical with conception, similitude, idea, genus, and species. Although we do not say that understanding and conceiving are identical, whatever things are understood and conceived are identical. What actually exists, however, is understood but not conceived from conversion.

PHILOSOPHER: What do you mean?

LAYMAN: Conceiving does not exist except as comprehension through the mode of matter or form or in some other way. What actually exists is said to be understood. That is, its peculiar nature is comprehended by the mind. Furthermore, the mind is said to understand that by which it is moved. It is better to call the beginning of the motion passion, while the intellect is said to be the perfection of the motion.[63] The passion of the mind is identical with the intellect in the same way that disposition and habit are identical; while disposition tends towards perfection, habit comes into existence after perfection is attained.

PHILOSOPHER: The intellect, however, does not seem to imply perfection.

LAYMAN: Well put. The mind, properly speaking, is said to understand when it is moved. But this is predicated of the intellect only with respect to perfection.[64]

PHILOSOPHER: All of the following are therefore identical: the power of conceiving, conception, similitude, idea, passion, and intellect.[65]

LAYMAN: They are identical, except that the power of conceiving is not any one of them. The reason for this is that the power of conceiving is named from the aptitude it has from its creation. Conception is named from imitation because it imitates matter or form. That is, it comprehends according to the mode of matter or form or their composite. Similitude or the idea of a thing is named according to the same rationale as conception. These names are truly said of one another. Each name is predicated of the intellect.

PHILOSOPHER: I wonder how conception can be called intellect.

LAYMAN: Although conception is named from imitation and the intellect from perfection, it is still perfection that causes the intellect to be called conception. For the mind conceives when the intellect is led to perfection.

PHILOSOPHER: Do you perhaps want to admit that the intellect is called the passion of the mind?

LAYMAN: I do, because the motion of the mind is the intellect. The beginning of this motion is a passion.

PHILOSOPHER: Is conception therefore also a passion?

LAYMAN: That does not follow, as you can see for yourself. Even though genera and species are similar to the intellect, they are not for that reason passions of the soul. A passion of the soul is transitory, but genera and species remain.

PHILOSOPHER: Enough of this. It suffices that I have heard you, since
     various men have spoken in different ways about these things.
     Tell me, though, how you name the power of the mind by which
     all things are intuited in the necessity of comprehension. And
     what is the other power called, by which all things are intuited in
     absolute necessity?

LAYMAN: As a layman I do not pay much attention to words. I do be-
     lieve, however, that the mind in considering its own immutability
     sees the forms of things extrinsic to matter through a power that
     is best called a discipline. It can be called this because the mind
     attains the consideration of form through discipline and doctrine.[66]
     The other power can be called intelligence because the mind, by
     means of it and in the intuition of its own simplicity, intuits all
     things in a simplicity abstracted from composition.

PHILOSOPHER: I have read that some men call intelligence what you
     call doctrine, and what you call intelligence, they call intelligibil-
     ity.

LAYMAN: This does not displease me since they can also be suitably
     named in this way.

ORATOR: Philosopher, I would like to hear how the philosophers of
     nature think that sensations occur. I believe that you are more
     experienced in this than the Layman, who will also be delighted
     if you will explain it.

PHILOSOPHER: I would be delighted to be able to relate something that
     I have learned. The explanation that you ask for is as follows. The
     philosophers of nature maintain that the soul is mixed with a very
     delicate spirit that is diffused through the arteries. Such a spirit
     is the vehicle of the soul.[67] The vehicle for this spirit, however, is
     the blood. There is, therefore, a particular artery, filled with this
     spirit, which is directed to the eyes. This artery divides in two
     near the eyes. Filled with spirit, it proceeds to the orbs of the eyes
     where the pupil is. This spirit is so diffused through the artery that
     it is an instrument of the soul, through which it administers the
     sense of seeing. Two arteries filled with this spirit are directed to
     the ears and to the nose as well as to the palate. This spirit is even
     diffused through the marrow to the extremities. The spirit that is
     directed to the eyes is the most agile. Therefore, when it meets
     some external object, it rebounds and the soul is stimulated to
     consider what is in the way. The spirit of the ears rebounds from
     a voice in a similar manner and the soul is stimulated to recognize

it. Hearing occurs in very refined air while smell requires air that is dense or more vaporous. Upon entering the nose, this air retards the spirit by its vapour so that the soul is stimulated to recognize the odour of the vapour. The spirit is impeded in a similar manner and the soul stimulated to taste when something moist and spongy enters the palate. The soul also employs the spirit that is diffused through the marrow as an instrument for touch. When something solid contacts the body, the spirit is affected and impeded in a certain manner. This is touch.

According to the order of the four elements, the power of fire is employed by the eyes. The power of ether, or more properly, pure air, is employed by the ears. The nose uses the power of dense and vaporous air, while the palate employs the power of water. The marrow uses the power of earth. Therefore, as the eyes are higher than the ears, the spirit that is directed to the eyes is higher and superior, with the result that to a certain extent it may be called fiery. It follows, then, that the disposition of the senses in man has been made similar to the order of the disposition of the four elements. Thus vision is more rapid than hearing. And even though they occur at the same time, we see lightning before we hear thunder. The direction of the rays of the eyes is so strong, subtle and acute that the air yields to it and nothing can resist it, except a mass of earth or water.

It is clear that nothing is sensed except through an obstacle. The reason for this is that this spirit is an instrument of the sense; the eyes, nose, and other senses are similar to windows and passageways, through which this spirit has a path that leads out to sensation. This spirit is an instrument of sensation. When it is hindered by something, the soul, as if impeded, may indistinctly comprehend the thing that hinders it by use of the senses.

Sense as it exists in itself, does not determine anything.[68] When we see something we determine it,[69] not by means of the senses, but through the faculty of imagination that is joined to sense. In the chamber of the imagination,[70] which is in the front part of the head, there is a spirit which is finer and more agile than one that is diffused throughout the arteries. The soul becomes more refined when it employs this spirit. Thus, even when a thing is absent, the soul still comprehends its form in the matter.[71] This power of the soul is called the imagination, because through it the soul conforms itself to the image of something absent. Con-

sequently, it is different from sense, which comprehends the form
in the matter only when a thing is present. Imagination does this
in the absence of a thing, but in a confused way. It therefore
does not discern the condition of a thing, but comprehends many
conditions in a confused way at the same time.

In the middle part of the head, namely in that chamber called
the rational, is the most delicate spirit. It is more refined than in
imagination. This spirit becomes even more refined when the soul
employs it as an instrument. Thus, it discerns one condition from
another, whether it be a condition or something formed. However,
because this spirit comprehends the forms mixed with matter, it
does not grasp the truth of things. For matter so disorders anything
that is formed that its truth cannot be comprehended. Nonetheless,
this power of the soul is called reason. The soul uses the corporeal
instrument in these three modes. It comprehends by itself when it
retains itself as an instrument, as we have learned from you.

ORATOR: Philosophers of nature are certainly to be praised for revealing these things to us according to experience. For they are
beautiful and pleasing things.

LAYMAN: This lover of wisdom also merits the greatest praise and
thanks.

Chapter IX. *How the mind measures all things by making the point,
the line and the surface. How the point is one and is the enfolding and
perfection of the line. Concerning the nature of enfolding. How the mind
produces adequate measures of the various things. What stimulates the
mind to this production.*

PHILOSOPHER: I see that night is approaching. You may therefore want
to proceed quickly to the many things that remain and explain how
the mind measures all things. You made this claim at the outset
of our discussion.

LAYMAN: The mind makes the point be the limit of the line and the
line be the limit of the surface and the surface be the limit of
the body.[72] It produces number and for this reason multitude and
magnitude proceed from the mind. Hence, the mind measures all
things.

PHILOSOPHER: Explain how the mind produces the point.

LAYMAN: The point is the intersection of one line with another, or the

limit of the line. Therefore, when you think of a line, the mind
will be able to consider the conjunction of the two halves with
each other. If this is done, there will be a line with three points,
because of its two ends and the conjunction of the halves that the
mind has proposed. The limits for the line and the conjunction
are not different kinds of points; the conjunction is truly the limit
of the two halves of the lines. If the mind were to postulate the
proper limit to each half, there would be a line with four points.
No matter how many parts a preconceived line is divided into
by the mind, there will be as many limits of the parts as the
preconceived line is judged to have points.

PHILOSOPHER: How does the mind make a line?

LAYMAN: It considers length without width, and surface with width
abstracted from solidity, even though neither point nor line nor
surface is able to exist in actuality. For only solidity can exist in
actuality, apart from the mind. The measure or limit of anything
is derived from the mind in this way: wood and stones have
a definite measure and limits that are beyond our mind. They
come from the uncreated mind, from which the limit of all things
descends.[73]

PHILOSOPHER: Do you think that the point is indivisible?

LAYMAN: I think that the limiting-point is indivisible, because there
is no limit for a limit. If it were divisible, it would not be a limit,
since it itself would have a limit. Thus it is not a quantity. Furthermore, quantity cannot be derived from points, because composites
are not able to be derived from that which is without quantity.

PHILOSOPHER: You agree with Boethius' dictum: "If you add a point to
a point, you do nothing more than if you join nothing to nothing."[74]

LAYMAN: If you join the ends of two lines, you will produce a longer
line, but joining the ends will produce no quantity.

PHILOSOPHER: Do you maintain that there are many points?

LAYMAN: There are neither many points nor many unities. Nevertheless, because the point is the limit of the line, it can be found
anywhere in the line. There is still but one point, however, which,
when extended, is the line.

PHILOSOPHER: Therefore, in truth, is nothing found in the line but the
point?

LAYMAN: Yes, but a certain extension is also present, because of the
variability of the matter that underlies it. Likewise, even though
there is but one unity, number is said to consist of many unities

resulting from the difference in the unity of the subjects. Consequently, the line is an evolution of the point, surface an evolution of the line, and a solid an evolution of the surface. It follows that if you take away the point, all magnitude ceases to exist. If you take away unity, every multitude ceases to exist.

PHILOSOPHER: How do you know that the line is an evolution of the point?

LAYMAN: Evolution is an unfolding, which is nothing more than the point existing in many atoms so that it is joined and continued in each one. One and the same point exists in all atoms, just as one and the same whiteness exists in all white things.

PHILOSOPHER: How do you know that the atom exists?

LAYMAN: According to the mind's consideration, a continuum is divided into that which is always divisible. The multiplicity increases to infinity, but in actuality the division arrives at a part that is actually indivisible, which I call the atom. The atom is a quantity that is actually indivisible because of its smallness. In the same way, a multitude has no end according to the mind's consideration. Still, it is limited in actuality. The multitude of all things falls under some determinate number, although it is not known to us.

PHILOSOPHER: Is the point the perfection of the line, being its limit?

LAYMAN: It is the perfection and totality of the line, which it enfolds in itself. For to punctuate[75] a thing is to limit it; at the place, however, where something is limited, it is brought to perfection, which is its totality. It follows then that the point is the limit, totality and perfection of the line, enfolding it in itself, just as the line unfolds the point. When I claim in geometry that the total perfection of the line exists from this point A to point B, I have designated through points A and B the totality of the line before it is drawn from A to B. That is, the line ought not to be drawn beyond them. Consequently, to enclose the totality of a thing, either in actuality or in the intellect, between this place and that, is to enfold the line in the point. To unfold it, however, is to draw the line consecutively from A to B. Accordingly, the line unfolds the enfolding of the point.

PHILOSOPHER: I thought that the point was the enfolding of the line in the same way that unity enfolds number. For nothing is found anywhere in the line but the point, just as nothing is found in number but unity.

LAYMAN: Your understanding of the issue is not bad. It is stating the same thing in a different manner of speaking. Your mode of discourse may be used for all enfoldings. Motion is the unfolding of rest, because nothing is found in motion but rest. The present instant[76] is unfolded through time, because nothing is found in time but the present instant. Likewise for all other things.

PHILOSOPHER: How do you account for nothing being discovered in motion but rest?

LAYMAN: When there is motion, there is a departure from one position to another. The reason for this is that a thing is not moved as long as it remains in the same position; hence nothing is found in motion but rest. Motion is a descent from one position. Consequently, movement is from one position to another position. To move, therefore, is to go from rest to rest. The result is that moving is nothing but ordered rest, or a series of ordered rests. He who seriously considers enfoldings and their unfoldings will profit greatly, particularly when he considers how the enfoldings are the images of the enfolding of infinite simplicity. They are its images, not its unfoldings, and they exist in the necessity of comprehension. The mind is the first image of the enfolding of the infinite simplicity. It enfolds the power of these enfoldings in its own power and is the place or region for the necessity of comprehension. The reason for this is that the things that really exist are abstracted from the variability of matter, being mental rather than material. I suspect that to mention this is superfluous.

ORATOR: It is in no way superfluous, even if it is repetitious. It is helpful to repeat often what cannot be discussed enough.

PHILOSOPHER: I wonder, Layman, why the mind strives so avidly to measure things, when, as you claim, its name (*mens*) is derived from measure (*mensura*).

LAYMAN: It strives to attain the measure of itself. The mind is a living measure that fulfills its own capacity by measuring other things. All that it does is for the sake of self-knowledge. Even though it seeks its measure in all things, it discovers it only where all things are one. That is where the truth of its precision exists, because that is where its adequate exemplar exists.

PHILOSOPHER: How is the mind able to make itself an adequate measure of such a variety of things?

LAYMAN: It can do this in the same way that an absolute face might make itself the measure of all faces. You will understand how the mind makes itself the idea, measure, or exemplar, so as to attain itself in all things, when once you observe that it is a particular and absolute measure that can be neither more nor less. It is not contracted to a quantity and yet is a living measure. Thus, it measures through itself as if it were a living circle[77] measuring through itself.

PHILOSOPHER: I realize that this simile is true for a circle of no determined quantity, because in order for determinations to be assimilated, the circle is both expanded and contracted. Explain, however, whether the mind assimilates itself to the modes of being.

LAYMAN: It does. The mind assimilates itself to all of them. For it conforms itself to possibility so as to measure all the things that possibly exist.[78] It conforms itself in the same way to absolute necessity so as to measure all things in unity and simplicity as God does. For the mind conforms itself not only to the necessity of comprehension, so as to measure all things in their proper being, but also to determinate possibility, so as to measure them according to the mode in which they exist. It measures figuratively by the mode of comparison. The mind does this when it uses number and geometrical figures, transforming itself into the similitude of such things. Therefore, to one who carefully observes, the mind is a living and uncontracted similitude of infinite equality.

Chapter X. How the comprehension of truth consists in multitude and magnitude.

PHILOSOPHER: Do not tire yourself, my friend, by continuing this discourse into the night. I wish to enjoy your company now, because I must leave tomorrow. Explain the saying of the most learned Boethius when he claims that the comprehension of the truth of all things is found in multitude and magnitude.[79]

LAYMAN: In my opinion he related multitude to discretion and magnitude to integrity.[80] For he who discerns something as existing in abstraction from all other things truly comprehends its truth. He attains the integrity of the thing, which does not proceed beyond or fall short of the integrity of its being. The discipline of geometry so determines the triangle that it exists neither beyond nor short of this integrity. Astronomy determines the integrity of motions and what each motion implies. Through the discipline of magnitude there is a limit and measure of the integrity of things, just as there is a discretion of things through the discipline of number. To be sure, number has the capacity for discerning the confusion of things that are common. Similarly, it collects things into a community. Magnitude is the result of the comprehension of the limit and measure of the integrity of the being of things.

PHILOSOPHER: If magnitude discerns the integrity of everything, then nothing is known unless everything is known.

LAYMAN: What you say is true. A part is not known unless the whole, which measures the part, is known. When I cut a spoon out of a piece of wood according to its parts, I consider the part, in so far as it must be, by adapting it to the whole. In doing this I may properly elicit a proportioned spoon. The whole spoon that I have conceived in my mind is thus an exemplar that I consider when I fashion a part.

When each part keeps its proportion as ordered to the whole, I am able to make a perfect spoon. In the same way, a part must conform to its integrity when it is compared to some other part. And so it will be necessary that knowledge of a whole and its parts will precede the knowledge of one part. Wherefore, if God, who is the exemplar of the universe, is not known, nothing clear is known about the universe. And if the universe is not known, nothing can be known of its parts. The knowledge of God and of all things thus precedes the knowledge of each thing.

PHILOSOPHER: Please explain also why he [Boethius] stated that no one should philosophize correctly without the quadrivium.[81]

LAYMAN: The reason is found in the things just mentioned. The power of numbers is contained in arithmetic and music, from which is derived the discretion of things. The discipline of magnitude is contained in geometry and astronomy, from which emanates the complete comprehension of the integrity of things. Therefore, no one ought to do philosophy without the quadrivium.

PHILOSOPHER: I wonder if he [Boethius] wanted to claim that everything that exists is either a magnitude or a multitude.

LAYMAN: I do not think that he wanted to claim this as much as he wanted to say that everything falls under either magnitude or multitude. The reason is that the demonstration of all things is made according to the power of one or the other of these concepts.[82] Magnitude limits and multitude discerns. Definition, which limits

and includes all being, has the power of magnitude and pertains
to it. The demonstration of definitions becomes a necessary definition according to the power of magnitude. Division and the
demonstration of divisions are made according to the power of
multitude. Demonstrations of syllogisms are made according to
the power of both magnitude and multitude. The deduction of a
third proposition from two others is due to multitude, while the
dependence of the conclusion upon universals and particulars is
the result of magnitude. With more leisure than we have, it might
be possible to show how quantity and quality as well as the other
categories that produce the ideas of things come from the power
of multitude. But it is difficult to realize how this might be done.

Chapter XI. *How all things exist in God in a trinity. The same is true in
our mind. How our mind is composed of the modes of comprehending.*

PHILOSOPHER: You dealt before with the Trinity of God and the trinity
    of our mind. I beg you now to explain how all things exist in God
    in a trinity and in the same fashion in our mind.
LAYMAN: You philosophers claim that the ten most general categories[83]
    embrace everything.
PHILOSOPHER: Indeed, that is so.
LAYMAN: Do you not see that they are divided when you consider
    them insofar as they actually exist?
PHILOSOPHER: By all means.
LAYMAN: When you consider them without division, prior to the be-
    ginning of their existence, what can they be other than eternity?
    Prior to all division, however, there is connection. Therefore, they
    had to be united and connected prior to all division. But the con-
    nection prior to all division is the most simple eternity, which is
    God. In addition, I claim that the universe of things exists in
    the perfection that is God, because it is not possible to deny that
    God is perfect, and what is perfect lacks nothing. The highest
    perfection demands that it be simple and one, without alterity and
    diversity. Thus all things in God are one.
PHILOSOPHER: You have presented a clear and pleasing account. But
    how are all things in a trinity?
LAYMAN: This matter should be treated elsewhere in order to be de-
    veloped more clearly. Nevertheless, so as to fulfill my promise

to explain, insofar as I am able, all the things that you demand, listen to this: you know that all the things that are in God from eternity are God. Consider then the universe of things in time. Because the impossible does not come into existence, do you not see that the universe could have been made from eternity?

PHILOSOPHER: The mind assents to this.

LAYMAN: You see in the mind, therefore, all things in their potential to be made.[84]

PHILOSOPHER: What you say is correct.

LAYMAN: And if they could be made, there had to have been the potential *to make*[85] prior to their existence.

PHILOSOPHER: Yes, there had to have been.

LAYMAN: Thus you see all things in the potential to make, prior to the temporal universe of things.

PHILOSOPHER: Yes.

LAYMAN: Was it not necessary that there be a connection of these two, potential to be made and potential to make, so that the universe of things that you see in your mind's eye in the absolute potential to be made and to make might advance into being? Otherwise, what could have been made through the power to make never would have been made.

PHILOSOPHER: Well put.

LAYMAN: You see, therefore, that all things in the connection prior to any temporal existence of things proceed from the absolute potential to be made and the absolute potential to make. Prior to all time, these three absolutes are simple eternity. Hence, you perceive in three ways all things in simple eternity.

PHILOSOPHER: Most sufficiently.

LAYMAN: Notice then how the absolute potential to be made, the absolute potential to make and the absolute connection are identical with one infinite absolute deity. The potential to be made is prior in the order of things to the potential to make. This is because making something presupposes the potential to be made. But the potential to make has what it possesses, which is the potential to make, from the potential to be made. Connection proceeds from both of these. Since order determines that the potential to be made takes precedence, unity, to which precedence belongs, is attributed to it. Equality presupposes unity and is attributed to the potential to make. From these comes connection. This should be enough about the topic, if you are satisfied.

PHILOSOPHER: Explain also if God understands as three and one.

LAYMAN: The eternal mind understands everything in unity, in equality of unity and in the connection of the two. How would God understand in eternity, in which there is no succession, except through being, the equality of being and the connection of the two, which is a trinity in unity? God would not bring something into the material mode of existence and then understand it in succession, as we do. His understanding, which is his essence, is necessarily in a trinity.

PHILOSOPHER: Explain if things are in our mind according to their own mode.

LAYMAN: All inchoate beings have a similitude of their principle in themselves. Consequently, I am convinced that a trinity in the unity of substances is found in all things having a similitude of the true trinity and the unity of the substance of the eternal principle. Therefore, in all inchoate beings there must be the following: the potential to be made, which descends from the infinite power of unity or absolute entity; the potential to make, which descends from the power of absolute equality; and the composition of both of these, which descends from absolute connection.

Consequently, our mind, the image of the eternal mind, engages in hunting its measure in the eternal mind as similitude engages in hunting its truth. For our mind, as a similitude of the divine mind, should be regarded as a high power in which the potential to be assimilated, the potential to assimilate and the connection of both are essentially identical. It follows that our mind, like the divine mind, can understand something only if it is one in trinity. When the mind first moves itself in order to understand, it presumes that there is something with a similitude to the potential to be made, which is matter. It unites with this something that has a similitude to the potential to make, which is form. The mind then understands according to the similitude of the composition of both. Its comprehension according to the material mode produces genera, according to the formal mode differences, and according to the composite mode species or individuals. As a result, when it understands according to the mode of a proper passion, it produces properties according to the mode of the contingent. These are the accidents. The mind understands nothing except what is presumed according to the material mode and the mode of the contingent form. It connects these in the mode of the composite.

In this succession, in which I have claimed that some things are presumed according to the modes of matter and form, you see that our mind understands as a similitude of the eternal mind. The eternal mind understands everything at the same time, without succession, and according to every mode of understanding. Succession, however, is a descent from eternity,[86] of which it is the image or similitude. Therefore, a mind that is united to a body subject to succession understands in succession. One should carefully observe that all things, as they exist in our mind, exist in a similar manner in matter, in form, and in the connection of the two.

PHILOSOPHER: What you say is very pleasing. But explain more clearly, I beg you, the matter which you advised us ought to be considered at the very end.

LAYMAN: With pleasure. Consider animal nature. The mind comprehends it at one time as a genus. This means that it considers the nature of animal according to the material mode, which is confused and uninformed. At another time, the mind considers it as it is signified by the name of animality; that is, according to the formal mode. At still another time, the mind considers it according to the mode of composition of the genus and the differences approaching it. On this occasion it is said to exist as connection in the mind. In this way the matter and the form, or rather the similitude of matter and form, and the mode of composition are considered to be one and the same idea, as well as one and the same substance.

Likewise, when I consider animal matter, humanity as the form approaching it, and the connection of the two, I claim that the matter, form, and connection are one substance. Or when I consider colour as matter, whiteness as the form approaching it, and the connection of the two, I claim that the matter, form, and the connection of the matter and the form are one and the same accident. The same is true for all things.

Do not be troubled by the fact that, when the mind produces the ten most general genera as the first principles, they have no common genus that could be posited as their matter. The reason for this is that the mind is able to consider a thing in the material mode and also according to the mode of the approaching form that comes to the matter. It is also able to do this with respect to the same thing according to the mode of composition, as when it considers the possibility of its being a substance or any other of the ten categories. It could reasonably be claimed that matter is the possibility of being a substance or an accident because the mind regards the approaching form and the matter as the same thing. Consequently, there may be a composition that is either a substance or any of the ten categories. These three then are one and the same most general category. In the universe of things that is the mind, all things exist in a trinity and in the unity of a trinity, according to the similitude of their existence in the eternal mind.

PHILOSOPHER: Do the ten most general categories not have these modes of existence separate from the mind's consideration?

LAYMAN: These ten most general categories are understood not as they exist in themselves, but as they exist in the mind according to the mode of form and the mode of composition. Yet they are considered to have these modes of existence in their subordinates. By precise observation you will notice that they are not able to exist in separation from the mind according to the formal and composite modes. You will especially notice this when you observe how quality can be said to be an accident when it exists in its subordinates, but not when it exists in itself. Thus it will be said that a particular condition, as it exists in the mind, perhaps cannot be considered in the material mode because the same particular and individual condition is considered first according to one mode and then according to another. We will say, therefore, that perhaps in itself it is not understood in the material mode but in its superiors.

PHILOSOPHER: I am satisfied with that. But I would like you to show me how things that actually exist are threefold as you mentioned earlier.

LAYMAN: It will be easy for you to see this if you attend to the fact that all things that actually exist do so in matter, form, and connection. The nature of humanity, insofar as it is the possibility of being a man, is matter. As humanity it is form; as a man it is the composition and connection of both. It is evident then that the possibility of being a man, the form, and the composition of the two are one and the same thing, such that there is one substance. In the same way, the nature that is designated by the term whiteness, as the possibility of being white, is matter. The form is that same whiteness, as is the composition of the two. Nonetheless, they exist in such a way that the matter, the form, and the composition of the two are by nature the same quality.

PHILOSOPHER: If being in matter is possible being, and possible being does not exist, how do all the things that actually exist, exist in matter?

LAYMAN: Do not be troubled by this. You will see that it can be understood without contradiction. I do not perceive that actual being contradicts what has existence in matter. Instead, one should understand that everything that actually exists—that is, as it exists here and in these things—certainly does not exist in matter. For example, the possibility of being a candle exists in wax and the possibility of being a pot exists in copper.

PHILOSOPHER: Please explain another matter: why is the Trinity said to be one individual?

LAYMAN: Because of the unifying unity in God, which is true substance. In other things it is due to the unity of nature, which is a kind of image of unifying unity and is properly a substance.

PHILOSOPHER: Why are both unity and equality said to be one?

LAYMAN: Because of the unity of substance.

PHILOSOPHER: But how is the Father one and the Son one when our theologians predicate unity of the Father, equality of the Son, and their bond of the Holy Spirit?[87]

LAYMAN: From the singularity of the person. There are three single persons in the one divine substance, as we have carefully discussed at another time as well as we were able.[88]

PHILOSOPHER: In order that I may understand what you said earlier, tell me if you believe that our mind is composed of these modes of comprehending. Furthermore, because our mind is a substance, will those modes be substantial parts of it? Tell me whether this is your opinion.

LAYMAN: As you mentioned earlier, Plato wanted to maintain that the mind is composed of indivisible and divisible substances. He took this notion from the modes of comprehension.[89] A thing known formally is comprehended without division. Thus, when the mind understands according to the formal mode, it comprehends without division. So we cannot truly speak of humanity as plural, but only of men, because a thing understood according to either the material mode or the mode of composition is understood by division. Our mind is a power of comprehension and a latent whole composed of all the powers of comprehension. Thus, every mode is verified by the whole mind, because it is a substantial part of it. It is difficult, I believe, to be able to say in what way the modes of comprehension are substantial parts of the power that is called the mind. Because the mind understands in one manner or another, the powers of the understanding, which are its parts, cannot be accidents. It is very difficult, however, to know and to express how they are substantial parts of the mind as well as being the mind itself.

PHILOSOPHER: Good Layman, help me a little with this difficult subject.

LAYMAN: The mind is virtually composed of the power of understanding, reason, imagination and sensation. The whole is consequently said to be the power of understanding, reason, imagination, and sensation. The mind is composed of these powers as out of its elements and it attains all things in its own mode in all things.[90] Because all things that actually exist are in the senses as in an indistinct mass and are distinguished by reason, they exist in actuality as they do in the mind, which is the most pronounced similitude for the mode of any being. The power of sensation in us is a power of the mind and thus is identical with the mind, just as every part of a line is the line itself. Magnitude, considered in itself apart from matter, is an appropriate example of what you have asked about. Each part of it is verified by the whole. Consequently, its being is identical with that of the whole.

PHILOSOPHER: If the mind is one, where do these powers of comprehension come from?

LAYMAN: They come from unity. What the mind understands as common to the material mode or the mode of composition, it possesses from unifying unity. Likewise, what it understands as singular, it possesses from unity, which is singularity. What it understands as formal, it has from unity, which is immutability. What it understands as divided, it has from unity, for division descends from unity.

Chapter XII. *How there is not one intellect in all men. How the number of independent minds, while innumerable to us, is known by God.*

PHILOSOPHER: I wish still to hear what you think about a few more things. Some of the Peripatetics maintain that there is one intellect in all men.[91] Others, who are Platonists, claim that there is not one intellectual soul. They say that our souls have an identical

substance with the world soul, which they claim is the comprehension of our souls.[92] Furthermore, they maintain that our souls
are numerically different because they have a different mode of
operation. Still, they say, the souls are reabsorbed into the world
soul after death. Tell me what you think about this problem.

LAYMAN: As you have heard before, I claim that the mind is the intellect. I do not, however, think that there is one mind in all men.
Because the mind has an operation by which it is called the soul,
it demands an appropriate relation to a body adequately proportioned to it. This relation is found in one body, but not in another
in the same way. Consequently, just as the identity of proportion
cannot be multiplied, neither can the identity of the mind. It is not
able to animate the body without an adequate proportion. Likewise, the vision of your eye could not be another's vision. Even
if it were separated from your eye and joined to another's eye, it
could not find in someone else's eye its own proportion. It finds
this only in your eye. The discretion that belongs to your vision
could not exist in another's vision. Similarly, the understanding
of this discretion could not be that of another's discretion.

Because of this, I do not believe that it is even possible for
one intellect to be in all men. The Platonists said that our souls
are resolved into one common soul that comprehends them. Perhaps the reason for this claim is the fact that number truly seems
to be removed when the variability of matter is taken away and
the nature of the mind outside of the body is free from all the
variability of matter, as was shown before. But I do not think that
such a resolution occurs.

Although we may not comprehend the multiplication of number removed from the variety of things, nevertheless their plurality
does not cease to exist. This plurality is a number in the divine
mind. Hence, the number of separate substances is no more a
number for us than non-number. To us it is innumerable and is
neither even nor odd, nor great nor small, nor does it agree with
any number that is denumerable by us. It is as though a man heard
a very loud shout from a great army of men and did not realize
that an army had uttered it. Obviously the different and distinct
voice of each man is in the shout that he hears, but the hearer has
no judgement of their number. As a result, he judges that it is
one voice, since he lacks a way to determine their number. Or if
many candles were burning in a room, which was illuminated by

all of them, the light of each candle would remain distinct from the light of the others. We prove this when one by one the candles are removed, taking their illumination with them. Assume then, that the candles burning in the room are extinguished but their illumination remains. If a man were to enter the room, he would see the brightness of the room, but would never apprehend the distinction and difference of the lights. In fact he could not be able to apprehend that there is a plurality of lights present, unless he knew that the lights were from extinguished candles. And even if he did know that there was a plurality, he still would not be able to distinguish by number one light from another.

You will be able to adduce similar examples for the other senses that could help you comprehend how the impossibility of numerical discretion exists with respect to a knowledge of plurality. Whoever observes how natures that are abstracted from all the variability of matter are intelligible to us without exception, sees that no creature can escape from the number of the divine mind. For if he considers these natures in relation to God, who alone is completely and infinitely absolute, he sees that they are not abstracted from every change, but are able to be changed and destroyed by Him, who alone dwells in immortality according to His nature.[93]

Chapter XIII. *How that which Plato called the world soul and Aristotle nature is God, who produces all things in all things.*[94] *How He creates the mind in us.*

PHILOSOPHER: So much for that question. What do you say about the world soul?

LAYMAN: Time does not permit us to investigate every question. I do think, however, that what Plato called the world soul, Aristotle called nature.[95] I conjecture that this soul or nature is nothing else than God producing all things in all things. We call this the spirit of the universe.

PHILOSOPHER: Plato claimed that this soul permanently contains the exemplars of things and moves all things. Aristotle said that nature moves all things wisely.

LAYMAN: Perhaps Plato wanted the world soul to be like the soul of a servant who knows the mind of his master and does his will. He called this knowledge the ideas or exemplars. They are not lost in oblivion, lest the completion of divine providence fail. And what Plato called the knowledge that belongs to the world soul, Aristotle wished to call the wisdom of nature, which is wisdom for carrying out God's orders. Because of this, they associate the necessity of comprehension with this soul or nature, since it must act in a determined manner as absolute necessity bids. But this is only a mode of understanding; it is similar to our mind's conception of God as the art of architecture, to which the art of construction is subordinate so that the divine concept might come into being. Because everything obeys an omnipotent will by necessity, the will of God does not require another being to carry it out. For willing and performing coincide in omnipotence, as when a glass blower makes glass. He blows his breath (*spiritus*) that accomplishes his will. In his breath exists word or conception as well as power. For if power and conception did not exist in the breath of the glass blower when he blows, no glass would come into being.

Imagine, therefore, an absolute creative art, subsisting in itself to such a degree that the art is the artist, and its mastery is the master. Nothing could resist such an art because its essence would necessarily include omnipotence. Likewise it would include wisdom so that it might know what it is doing. Furthermore, it would possess the connection of omnipotence and wisdom so that what it wills might be accomplished. This connection, having in itself both wisdom and omnipotence, is spirit, which is either will or desire. It is not possible for there to be either the will or the desire for things that are impossible and totally unknown.

It follows that wisdom and omnipotence exist in the most perfect will, and is called spirit from a certain similitude. Since without spirit there is no motion, we call that which produces motion in the wind and in all other things spirit.[96] All artists produce what they wish through movement. The power, therefore, of a creative art that is an absolute and infinite art, or the blessed God, produces all things. It does this by means of a spirit or will in which the wisdom of the Son and the omnipotence of the Father dwell. The result is that its work is that of one undivided Trinity.

The Platonists had not known[97] this connection, spirit, or will because they did not see that this spirit is God. They supposed that it had come from God and was a soul animating the world, as our intellective soul animates our body.[98] The Peripatetics also failed to understand this spirit; they posited this force as a nature immersed in things, from which comes motion and rest, even though it is the absolute deity blessed in eternity.

ORATOR: How pleased I am when I hear so clear an explanation. But I beg you once more to give an example that might help us understand the creation of our mind in our body.

LAYMAN: You have heard about this before, but a variety of examples does make the inexpressible clearer. You know that our mind is a certain power that has the image of divine art. This has already been described. Consequently, all the things that the divine art contains in perfect truth exist truly in our mind as its image. As a result, the mind is created by the art of the creator as if the art sought to create itself.

But because the infinite art is not able to be multiplied, its image arises. It is like a painter who wished to depict himself; because he himself cannot be multiplied, only his image arises through his painting. If an image, no matter how perfect, cannot be more perfect and more conformable to its exemplar, it is not as perfect as an imperfect image having the potential of conforming itself more and more, without limit, to the inaccessible exemplar. This image imitates infinity in the only way in which it can. It is as if a painter made two images. One image actually would appear to be more like him, but is lifeless. The other image, although less like him, is alive in such a way that it can make itself even more like the painter when it is stimulated to motion by its object. No one would doubt that the second painting is more perfect, since it comes closer to the art of the painter. So our mind, indeed every mind, has from God a mode in which it is able to be a perfect and living image of the infinite art, even though it may be created lower than all other minds.

The mind is thus both three and one, having power, wisdom, and the connection of both in such a way that it is a perfect image of this art. When it is stimulated it is always able to conform itself more and more to its exemplar. Our mind has a certain created power, which when aroused allows it to make itself more like the actuality of the divine art, even though at the beginning of its creation it has no actual splendour[99] of the creative art in trinity and unity. Power, wisdom, and volition exist, therefore, in the unity of the mind's essence, where the teacher and the teaching coincide as a living image of the infinite art.[100] Once this image is stirred, it can always without limits conform itself more closely to the divine actuality, even though the precision of the infinite art remains inaccessible forever.

ORATOR: Wonderfully and very clearly spoken. Explain however, how the mind is infused by creation.

LAYMAN: You have heard about this before. Listen now to another example.

The Layman took a glass, held it up between his thumb and finger, and struck it. It gave off a sound that continued for a while. Then he shattered the glass and the sound ceased. The Layman continued speaking.

Through my power, a certain force came into being in the suspended glass. It moved the glass and from this motion a sound arose. When the proportion of the glass, in which the motion and the consequent sound resided, was shattered, the motion ceased, as did the sound. If this power did not depend upon the glass, and consequently did not cease, but continued without the glass, then you would have an example of how that power is created in us that produces motion and harmony. It stops doing this when the proportion is broken, even though it does not cease to exist on that account. If I teach you the art of playing the zither on a given instrument, the art would not depend upon the particular zither, even though you learned on it. If the instrument were destroyed, the art of playing does not perish, even if no zither suitable for you could be found in the world.

Chapter XIV. How the mind is said to descend and return through the planets to the body from the Milky Way.[101] Concerning the indestructible ideas of the pure spirits[102] and our changeable ideas.

PHILOSOPHER: You produce very appropriate and beautiful examples for things that are rare and remote from the senses. But sunset now approaches and leaves us little time. So please explain what philosophers have in mind when they say that souls descend from the Milky Way through the planets into bodies and return to it in the same way. And when Aristotle wanted to describe the power of our soul, why did he begin with reason, claiming that the soul ascends from reason to science and from science to intelligibility? Why did Plato say just the opposite, maintaining that intelligibility is the first principle and that it becomes science or intelligence by a degeneration and then degenerates further to become reason?

LAYMAN: I do not know their writings. It may be, however, that the first man who spoke about the descent and ascent of souls wanted to maintain the same thing as Plato and Aristotle. Plato, in contemplating the image of the creator, saw that it is at its greatest in intelligibility. He posited the first principle and substance of the mind in this intelligibility, where the mind conforms itself to the divine simplicity. For he intended the mind to survive after death.

This intelligibility precedes intelligence in the order of nature. It degenerates into intelligence, however, when it departs from the divine simplicity, where all things are one, and wishes to see all things in themselves, where each thing possesses its own proper being distinct from any other. The mind continues to degenerate when, through the motion of reason, it comprehends a thing as a form existing in changeable matter and not as it is in itself. Here the mind is not able to grasp truth, but inclines toward an image. Aristotle, however, considered all things insofar as they were subject to designation, which is imposed by the motion of reason. He made reason the first principle. Perhaps he also claimed that reason ascends to intelligence through discipline, which is the result of designation. Afterwards it ascends even higher to the intelligible. Thus he posited reason as the first principle for the ascent of the intellect. Plato chose intelligibility for its descent. So there does not seem to be any difference between them, except in the mode of consideration.

PHILOSOPHER: What you say may be true. But how is it true of God and of prime matter, when every philosopher says that all understanding is concerned with substance and accident?

LAYMAN: The understanding of God is derived from the understanding of the term "being." This is because God is understood as a being of not-being, which is a being that cannot be participated. This understanding is the same as the understanding that we possess of substance and accident. It is, however, considered in a different mode, which is that of derivation. Thus, the understanding of God is a complex of every understanding of substance and accident. Yet it is simple and one. The understanding of prime matter is a certain derivation of an understanding of body. If you have an incorporeal understanding of a body separated from any corporeal form, you understand what the word "body" signifies, but in a different mode because it is incorporeal. This is without a doubt an understanding of matter.

PHILOSOPHER: Do you think that the celestial minds[103] were created according to intellectual degrees and have eternal ideas?

LAYMAN: I think that there are intellectual angels,[104] as are those of the highest order. Those of the second order are intelligences, while those of the third order are rational. Within each order there are just as many degrees. Thus there are nine degrees or choirs.[105] Our minds are below the lowest grade of these spirits and above every grade of corporeal nature; for our minds are a sort of connection of the universe of beings in the sense that they are the limit of perfection for lower natures and the beginning of the higher natures. In addition, I think that the ideas in the blessed spirits, who exist peacefully outside the body, are immutable and not subject to extinction through forgetfulness. This is because of the presence of the truth, which offers itself to them objectively and without interruption. This is the reward for spirits who deserved the enjoyment of the exemplars of things. Even though our minds have been created with a permanent aptitude to renew their knowledge of things, they often forget what they have known because of their deformity.

Regardless of the fact that our minds' intellectual progress can be stimulated only through the body, the minds' ideas can be lost because of negligence, lack of attention to their object, the distraction of changeable and diverse things, and corporeal cares. The ideas that we acquire in this variable and unstable world are uncertain because we acquire them according to the conditions of a changing world. They are similar to the ideas of scholars and students who are beginning to make progress, but who are not yet brought to the mastery of learning. These acquired ideas, however, are transformed into an unchangeable mastery when the mind proceeds from the changeable to the unchangeable world. For when particular ideas are transformed into a perfect mastery of doctrine, those ideas that were the most mutable and unstable cease to be changeable within the universal mastery. Consequently, we are students capable of being taught while we are in this world. In the other world we shall be masters.

Chapter XV. *How our mind is immortal and incorruptible*

PHILOSOPHER: There is enough time remaining for you to tell me your
opinion about the immortality of our mind. I shall then possess
as much instruction concerning the mind as is possible to attain
in one day and I shall rejoice in having made progress in many
things.

LAYMAN: Those who posit intelligibility as the principle of the descent of the intellect claim that the mind in no way depends on
the body. On the other hand, those who posit reason as the principle of the ascent of the intellect, and intelligibility as its end,
admit that in no way does the mind perish with the body. I do not
hesitate to say that those who have a taste of wisdom are unable
to deny the mind's immortality. I have already told the Orator the
things that have occurred to me about this topic. The intuition of
the mind attains the unchangeable. Through the mind, forms are
abstracted from variability and restored to the changeless region
of the necessity of comprehension. Those who see these things
cannot doubt that the nature of the mind is free from all variability,
for the mind draws to itself what it abstracts from variability. The
unchangeable truth of geometrical figures is found in the mind,
not on the pavement.[106]

When the soul inquires by means of the organs, it finds that
which is changeable, but when it inquires through itself, it finds
that which is stable, clear, bright, and determined. Thus, its nature
is not composed of the changeable things that it attains through
sensation, but of those changeless things that it finds in itself.

The demonstration of its immortality can be suitably sought
after in this way in number: the number of our mind cannot
be conceived as being corruptible because it is a living number,
which is a number that enumerates. Every number is incorruptible
in itself, even though it may appear to be changeable when it is
considered in relation to changeable matter. How then could the
author of number appear to be corruptible? Nor is any number
able to exhaust the power of an enumerating mind. Thus, because
the motion of the heavens is enumerated by the mind and time is
the measure of motion, time will never exhaust the power of the
mind. The mind remains the limit, measure, and determination
of all measurable things. The instruments for measuring celestial
motions proceed from the human mind. They reveal that the mind

measures motion more than motion measures the mind. It follows that the mind appears to enfold all successive motion through its own intellectual motion. The mind produces from itself a syllogistic motion. It is therefore a form of motion. Consequently, if something is destroyed, it happens through motion.

How then could the form of motion be destroyed through motion? The mind, because it is an intellectual life that moves itself, is a life that produces its own understanding. How could it help but live forever? How does self-motion fail? It has life joined together with it, through which it is always alive. It is similar to the sphere: it is always round due to the circle that is joined to it. If the mind is composed out of itself, as number is, how can it be resolved into that which is not mind? As a result, if the mind, like number, is the coincidence of unity and difference, how can it be divisible, since divisibility coincides with the indivisible unity in it? If the mind enfolds both identity and difference, because it understands through distinction and union, how will it be destroyed? If the mind's mode of understanding is numerical, and unfolding coincides with enfolding in its enumeration, how will the mind perish? For a power that enfolds by means of unfolding is not able to become less. The mind, however, appears to do this.

Whoever enumerates, unfolds the power of unity as well as enfolding number in unity. A denarius is a unity enfolded from ten. It follows that whoever enumerates both unfolds and enfolds. The mind is an image of eternity, and time is its unfolding. The unfolding, however, is always less than the image of the enfolding of eternity. Whoever attends to the judgement created in the mind, through which it judges all things, will notice that reasons come into being because of the mind. He will observe that no reason reaches the measure of the mind. Thus, our mind remains immeasurable, timeless, and beyond definition to every reason. Only the uncreated mind measures, limits, and determines its own end, just as truth does with respect to its own living image that is created from it, in it, and through it. How would the image perish, which is an incorruptible reflection of truth, unless the truth abolish the reflection that was communicated? And so, just as it is not possible for infinite truth, because of its absolute goodness, to withdraw the reflection that has been communicated, so it is likewise impossible for its image, which is nothing but its communicated reflection, ever to perish. Similarly, when day has begun, caused by the reflection of the sun, it will not cease as long as the sun is shining.

During this year the innate sense of religion, which has attracted this innumerable crowd of people to Rome, has also attracted you, Philosopher, who come filled with great wonder. This sense of religion has always appeared diversely in the world. It shows that the immortality of our mind is given to us by nature with the result that it is as manifest to us from the certain and universal assertion of all men as is the humanity of our nature. For we are no more certain of our humanity than of the immortality of our minds, even though the knowledge of both is a universal claim of all men. Accept willingly these things that have been described in haste by a layman. If they are not what the promise of the Orator had led you to expect, they still are something that perhaps will be able to offer you some aid for higher things.

ORATOR: Having been present during this holy and most pleasing discussion, I greatly admire the profound discourse of your mind about the mind. Because of this experience I do not doubt that the mind has a definite power to measure all things. Thank you, good Layman, both on my behalf and on that of this visiting philosopher whom I brought. I hope he will depart consoled.

PHILOSOPHER: I do not believe that I have lived a day more blessed than this one. I do not know what will follow, but I give thanks to both of you: to you Orator, and to you Layman, who are a man of profound contemplation. I pray that, stimulated to a wondrous desire by this long discussion, our minds may be drawn in bliss to the enjoyment of the eternal mind. Amen.

END OF THE THIRD BOOK OF THE LAYMAN

NOTES

1 The Jubilee of 1450.

2 Aristotle, *Metaphysics* I, 2; Plato, *Theatetus* 155d; *Phaedrus* 250a; Cusanus, *Excitationes* IX (Paris ed.), II, 167r.

3 Cf. Plato, *Philebus* 48c; *Phaedrus* 229e.

4 *Mens* (Mind) was the goddess of thought. Cf. N. Hammond and H. H. Scullard, *The Oxford Classical Dictionary* (Oxford, 1973), p. 672. It was T. Octacilius who dedicated the temple. Cicero mentions a shrine to Mens dedicated by M. Aemilius Scaurus. Cf. *De natura deorum* II, 61. He also mentions a companion shrine dedicated to *Fides* (faith).

5 "into error" added.

6 *Coniectura*. This is the technical term Cusanus uses to indicate the nature of finite human knowledge. Cf. *De coniecturis* I, ch. 11.

7 *Perfectus*.

8 "Mentem a mensurando dici." Cusanus may have found this etymology in St. Augustine, *De trinitate* VI, ix, 12.

9 *Complicatur*.

10 Proclus, *Elements of Theology*, prop. 195. *Liber de causis*, prop. 14 (Bardenhewer 176.8 sq.).

11 *Imponenti* refers to the imposition of designation.

12 *Complicat*.

13 Cf. *De docta ig.* I, 14, p. 28.

14 *Metrum*. It is not clear what the difference is between *metrum* and *mensura* in Cusanus' Latin.

15 Cusanus is referring to the sense-image of something intelligible.

16 Plotinus, *Enneads* I, 6, 8, and 9.

17 *Coclearitas*.

18 Seneca, *Epistles* LXV.

19 *Resplendeo* is often used by the medieval Neoplatonists to emphasize the relation between the creator and the creature in terms of the image of the illumination of light.

20 *Adventu*.

21 *Motus rationis*.

22 *In mentis intelligentia*.

23 J. Kroll. *Die Lehren des Hermes Trismegistos* (Münster, 1914) 40, 44.

24 St. Augustine, *De trinitate* XIV, 8.

25 *Productio* should be rendered as "bringing forth" in order to retain the Neoplatonic language of the spontaneous emanation of things.

26 Proclus, *Elements of Theology*, prop. 174.

27 Giordano Bruno, *De la causa, principio e uno*, Dialog V (*opp. Ital.*, I, pp. 249, 258.)

28 The term "connate" is preferred to "innate" as a rendering of the Latin *concreata* because it shares the same Latin prefix denoting simultaneity.

29 Aristotle, *De anima* 429a23.

30 Plato, *Phaedo* 72c.

31 Cf. Plato, *Republic* 507b.

32 *Ibid.* 523b–c. Cusanus appears to be referring directly to the Platonic text.

33 *Intelligere* = understanding.

34 Cf. St. Augustine, *De magistro*, ch. 11, 12.

35 The Latin word for soul (*anima*) is related to the verb "to animate" (*animare*).

36 Cf. Plato, *Phaedrus* 246a and c; *Timaeus* 34c.

37 Cf. 1 John 3, 9: "Semen ipsius in eo manet." Perhaps Cusanus has Meister Eckhart's *Von dem edlen Menschen* in mind.

38 *Vita intellectiva*.

39 *Resplendentia* refers to the reflection of light as either process or product. Cf. n. 19, ch. 2 above.

40 Plotinus, *Enneads* VI, 6. Cusanus may have also encountered the formula in Macrobius' *Commentary on the Dream of Scipio* I, 14, 19.

41 In medieval Latin *mathematicus* tends to be equivalent to the terms "abstract" or "theoretical." This seems consistent with Cusanus' usage throughout the chapter.

42 *Primum principiatum*. This refers to the first being brought into existence by the infinite principle. Cf. Aristotle, *Metaphysics* 985b31.

43 Reading *singillatim* (separately) instead of *sigillatim* (under a seal). There is justification for this reading in the ms tradition of the text.

44 The preceding two passages are rather obscure. The translation attempts to present a reading that Cusanus may have intended.

45 Notice that Cusanus wishes to refer to a class of numbers and not to any specific numbers. According to his analysis, a ternary number might be 3 (=2 + 1), 5 (=4 + 1), 7 (=6 + 1), and so on.

46 It is not clear why Cusanus suddenly shifts from mind (*mens*) to spirit (*animus*) in this passage.

47 Following St. Bonaventure, Cusanus uses the term *vestigium* to indicate a sign by means of which the soul can journey back to God. Unlike St. Bonaventure, who places *vestigia* outside of the human knower in corporeal reality, Cusanus argues that the principle *vestigium*, the sign or path leading us back to God (*ducens in sapientiam*), is number, an exemplar both in our mind and in the mind of God.

48 *Aliae et discretae*.

49 *Ita de aliis*. Cusanus is referring to the ten Aristotelian categories.

50 *Unitas uniens*.

51 Dionysius, *Div. nom.* V, 8.

52 *Alteritas*.

53 Cusanus may have found these theories in Macrobius, *Commentarium in*

somnium Scipionis I, 14, 19. Notice that Cusanus is taking up a proposition that he stated at the beginning of the last chapter.

54 Cusanus may have Meister Eckhart's doctrine of the *scintilla animae* (spark of the soul) in mind here. He is also developing an argument against the Averroistic doctrine of the unicity of the intellect. Cf. E. Cassirer, *The Individual and the Cosmos in Renaissance Philosophy* (New York, 1964) 130–131.

55 *Entificativa.*

56 Reading *imaginatio* (imagination) instead of *imago* (image).

57 Cf. Albertus Magnus, *De creatione*, q. 78. Alcher of Clairvaux, *De spiritu et anima*, ch. 33.

58 *Modus in possibilitate essendi seu materia, modus possibilitas essendi per formam determinata.* Cf. Aristotle, *Metaphysics* 1032a21–24.

59 Cusanus is referring to the paving stones of a floor, used no doubt as a convenient blackboard.

60 *In necessitate complexionis.* The wide range of meanings of *complexio* makes this phrase difficult to translate. Since the context indicates a form of mathematical or logical necessity that the mind can grasp, "necessity of comprehension" seems preferable to renderings such as "necessity of connection."

61 *Intuetur.*

62 *Posse-esse.*

63 Cusanus is referring to the Aristotelian distinction between the active and passive intellect.

64 *Nisi post perfectionem.* Cusanus is ambiguous here. Perhaps he means to say that the intellect is not said to understand until after it has attained its perfection, namely the object that it understands.

65 The terms "passion" and "intellect" refer to the passive and the active intellects respectively. The term "passion" should not be identified only with the irrational faculties.

66 Discipline (*disciplina*) implies learning and doctrine (*doctrina*) teaching.

67 Cf. Boethius, *De consolatione philosophiae* III, poem ix, 19, 28; Proclus, *Elements of Theology*, prop. 205; Aristotle, *De generatione animalium* 736b32.

68 *Nihil terminat.*

69 *Terminum in ipso ponimus.*

70 *Cellula phantastica.* Cf. Alcher of Clairvaux, *op. cit.*, ch. 33; Albertus Magnus, *op. cit.*, q. 38, 3.

71 Cf. A. Schneider, *Die Psychologie Alberts der Grossen* (Münster, 1903/1906), Vol. I, pp. 164, 178.

72 Cf. Euclid, *Elements*, Bk. I, defs. 3, 6 and 14.

73 *Descendit.* The language is Neoplatonic. Cusanus analyzes this language in his *De dato patris luminum*. Cf. Proclus' *The Elements of Theology*,

prop. 117.

74 Boethius, *De arithmetica* II, 4.

75 *Punctare*. Literally it means to make a point.

76 *Nunc.*

77 *Circinus* may also refer to the compass that is used to draw a circle.

78 *Possibiliter mensuret*. This phrase is difficult to render. Another version might be, "to measure all things as well as possible."

79 Boethius, *De arithmetica* I, 1.

80 *Ibid.* II, 3. Cusanus interprets the Boethian quadrivium as follows:

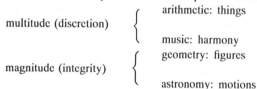

multitude (discretion) { arithmetic: things / music: harmony

magnitude (integrity) { geometry: figures / astronomy: motions

For a general study of the quadrivium in the Middle Ages see William Harris Stahl, *Martianus Capella and the Seven Liberal Arts* (New York, 1971), Pt. III, "The Quadrivium," pp. 123–228.

81 Boethius, *op. cit.* I, 1.

82 Boethius, *In Isagogen Porphyrii commenta* I, 9.

83 Cf. Aristotle, *The Categories*.

84 *Posse-fieri* is literally rendered as "to be able to be made."

85 *Posse-facere* is rendered as "to be able to make."

86 This is a Neoplatonic idea.

87 St. Augustine, *De doctrina christiana* I, v.

88 Cf. Cusanus, *De docta ig.* I, 7.

89 Cf. Plato, *Timaeus* 35a.

90 Cusanus' Latin is ambiguous. An alternative reading would be "it attains all things in its own mode in all these powers."

91 This doctrine came to the West through Averroes' *Commentarium magnum in Aristotelis de anima libros*, III, comm. 4, 5, 19. The doctrine was condemned at Paris in 1270 and again in 1277.

92 Cf. Plato, *Timaeus* 41d–e.

93 Cf. 1 Tim. 6, 16.

94 For a good analysis of the problem discussed in this chapter see Tullis Gregory, *Anima Mundi* (Florence, 1955), ch. 3, "L'anima del mondo e l'anima individuale," and ch. 4, "L'idea di natura."

95 Plato, *Timaeus* 41d; Aristotle, *Metaphysics* 1014b.

96 *Spiritus* can mean breath as well as spirit. Cusanus takes advantage of this double meaning in this passage and above where he talks about the glass blower.

97 Reading *ignorarent* instead of *ignorarant*.

98 Cf. Plato, *Timaeus* 34–35.

99 This term may also be rendered as "reflection."
100 Cf. St. Augustine, *De magistro*, ch. 14.
101 Cusanus most likely encountered this idea in Macrobius' *Commentary on the Dream of Scipio* I, ch. 12.
102 *Spirituum separatorum.*
103 The problem of the celestial intelligences is expressed well in Albertus Magnus, *Summa de creaturis*, Ia, tract. iii, q. 16, art. 2.
104 Reading *intellectuales* instead of *intellectibiles*.
105 Cf. Dionysius, *De cael. hier.*, ch. 6.
106 Cf. n. 59, ch. VII above.

Bibliography

Modern Editions of Cusanus' Writings:

Opera omnia. Ed. iussu et auct. Acad. Heidelbergensis (1932—present).
Philosophish-Theologische Schriften. Ed. Leo Gabriel. 3 Vols. Vienna, 1967.
Der Laie über die Weisheit. German translation by E. Bohnenstädt. Leipzig, 1935.
Der Laie über den Geist. German translation by M. Honecker and H. Menzel-Rogner. Hamburg, 1949.

Secondary Literature Relevant to Cusanus' Idiota:

Bett, H. *Nicholas of Cusa.* London, 1932.
Biechler, J. E. *The Religious Language of Nicholas of Cusa.* Missoula, 1975.
Bohnenstädt, E. "Zu des Nikolaus von Kues' Schrift *Über die Weisheit.*" *Forschungen und Fortschritte* 12 (1936) 169–170.
Cranz, F. E. "Cusanus, Luther, and the Mystical Tradition." *Studies in Medieval and Reformation Thought.* Ed. H. Oberman. Leiden, 1974. Vol. X.
_____ . "Saint Augustine and Nicholas of Cusa in the Tradition of Western Christian Thought." *Speculum* 28 (1953) 297–316.
Duclow, D. F. "Gregory of Nyssa and Nicholas of Cusa: Infinity, Anthropology and the Via Negativa." *The Downside Review* 92 (1974) 102–108.
Führer, M. L. "Purgation, Illumination and Perfection in Nicholas of Cusa." *The Downside Review* 98 (1980) 169–189.
_____ . "Wisdom and Eloquence in Nicholas of Cusa's *Idiota de sapientia et de mente.*" *Vivarium* 16 (1978) 142–155.
Rice, E. "Nicholas of Cusa's Idea of Wisdom." *Traditio* 13 (1957) 345–368.
_____ . *The Renaissance Idea of Wisdom.* Cambridge, MA, 1958.
Seigel, J. E. *Rhetoric and Philosophy in Renaissance Humanism.* Princeton, 1968.
Stadelmann, R. *Vom Geist des ausgehenden Mittelalters.* Halle/Saale, 1929.
Vansteenberghe, E. *Le Cardinal Nicholas de Cues. 1401–1464.* Paris, 1920.
Vasoli, C. *La dialettica e la retorica dell'Umanesimo.* Milan, 1968.

Publications
of the
Centre for Reformation and Renaissance Studies
Victoria University
Toronto

Occasional Publications:

OP1 *Humanist Editions of the Classics at the CRRS.*
Compiled by N.L. Adamson et al. (1979), ix, 71 pages.

Out of print.

OP2 *Humanist Editions of Statutes and Histories at the CRRS.*
Compiled by Konrad Eisenbichler et al. (1980), xxi, 63 pages.

$6.00

OP3 *Bibles, Theological Treatises and Other Religious Literature, 1492–1700, at the CRRS.*
Compiled by Konrad Eisenbichler et al. (1981), viii, 94 pages.

$6.00

OP4 *Published Books (1499–1700) on Science, Medicine and Natural History at the CRRS.*
Compiled by William R. Bowen and Konrad Eisenbichler (1985), ix, 35 pages.

$6.00

OP5 *Language and Literature. Early Printed Books at the CRRS.*
Compiled by William R. Bowen and Konrad Eisenbichler (1986), ix, 112 pages.

$6.00

OP6 *Register of Sermons Preached at Paul's Cross (1534–1642).*
Compiled by Millar MacLure. Revised and expanded by Peter Pauls and Jackson Campbell Boswell (1989), 151 pages.

$8.00

Translation Series:

TS1 Lorenzo Valla, *The Profession of the Religious* and the principal arguments from *The Falsely-Believed and Forged Donation of Constantine.*
Trans. Olga Zorzi Pugliese (1985), 74 pages.

$6.00

TS2 Giovanni della Casa, *Galateo.*
Trans. Konrad Eisenbichler and Kenneth R. Bartlett (1986), 83 pages.

$6.00

TS3 Bernardino Ochino, *Seven Dialogues.*
Trans. Rita Belladonna (1988), 96 pages.

$8.00

Distribution

Dovehouse Editions Inc.
32 Glen Ave.
Ottawa, Canada
K1S 2Z7